Elie Wiesel: Witness for Life

Elie Wiesel: Witness for Life

by ELLEN NORMAN STERN

KTAV PUBLISHING HOUSE, INC.
NEW YORK
1982

© Copyright 1982
Ellen Norman Stern

Library of Congress Cataloging in Publication Data

Stern, Ellen Norman.
 Elie Wiesel, witness for life.

 Bibliography: p.
 1. Wiesel, Elie, 1928-   —Biography.
2. Authors, French—20th century—Biography.
3. Jewish authors—Biography. 4. Holocaust
survivors—Biography. I. Title.
PQ2683.I32Z88   813'.54   81-23683
ISBN 0-87068-766-2   AACR2
ISBN 0-87068-767-0 (pbk.)

Cover from photograph of Elie Wiesel by Dr. Roman Vishniac

Manufactured in the United States of America

For
LARRY AND MICHAEL

Acknowledgments

My friend Joyce Kutler was responsible for my introduction to the writings of Elie Wiesel. I remember well her book reviews of the early Wiesel books and her conviction that his was a great talent with an urgent message to transmit. Joyce lent me many of her notes and newspaper clippings for use in the preparation of this manuscript. Above all, she has, throughout the years, given me her steady support and encouragement for which I will always be grateful.

I wish to thank Mordecai Shualy of Baltimore, who shared with me his memories of the Wiesel family, and who painted a vivid picture of the town of Sighet, in which he and his friend Elie grew up. The hospitality and friendship I received in the home of Mordecai and Frieda Shualy left a warm glow.

Their son, Moshe Dov Shualy of Philadelphia, has been a source of much information about the deeply religious milieu from which Elie Wiesel came. I am appreciative of all I learned from Moshe and uplifted by his belief that my project was "sacred work."

Mrs. Mildred Kurland has again been most helpful to me. As librarian of Congregation Rodeph Shalom, Philadelphia, she was aware that I borrowed every Wiesel book and newsclipping in her library for an unconscionable length of time, yet she never pushed me to return any of it. Every writer needs a librarian friend such as she.

Dr. Harry James Cargas of Webster College, St. Louis, compiled a book, *In Conversation with Elie Wiesel* (Paulist Press), which contains a goldmine of biographical information. Not only do I wish to thank him for putting out that book, but also for his generosity in permitting me to use material and quotations from it in this manuscript. His kindness has made my task easier.

Professor Nora Levin of Gratz College, Philadelphia, has read and reviewed my manuscript. Her suggestions, based on her vast and authoritative knowledge of Holocaust materials, were accepted and acted on wherever possible. I thank her for her kindness to me and for her continuing interest in the progress of this book.

Were it not for Mr. Bernard Scharfstein of KTAV Publishing House this book would not have been written by me at all. It was Bernie's suggestion that I write about Elie Wiesel and he has my thanks for his patience in seeing me through the numerous ups and downs which accompanied this project. I wish to express my sincere thanks to Mr. Irving Ruderman for his diligent work on this book.

I am grateful to Mr. Robert Milch for his able copy editing of the manuscript. His skill and understanding guided me through the difficult period when much material needed to be cut. His encouragement came at a time when I needed it most.

To the many others who have taken an interest and helped me during the writing of this book I offer a heartfelt "thank you."

It is important to state that this story about Elie Wiesel is not, and was never intended to be, a definitive or critical biography. From personal interviews with him and from a reading of his works, certain impressions and feelings have filtered through me. These interpretations are strictly my own.

The author gratefully acknowledges permission to reprint material from the following books by Elie Wiesel:
Night. Translated from the French by Stella Rodway. ©

Preface

"Permit me to tell you a story."

These are the words Elie Wiesel often uses to begin an evening's lecture or one of his college "encounters."

Why am I borrowing these words? Because they tell best how it happened that I was destined to write a story about this man who has become the prophet of his generation, which is also mine.

A long time ago when I was a little girl pushing a doll carriage along the sidewalk of my Berlin street, a young boy my age sat listening to stories in the House of Study of his hometown in the heart of Central Europe. We were far apart in location, background, and upbringing, yet, without our knowing it, a common experience was being prepared for us which would affect both his future and mine. We did not sense the coming of this experience, for we were both still living in the world of childhood, where all bad stories have happy endings.

Then the whirlwind came. Nothing remained the same.

Destiny was kind to me. I was allowed to live and to grow up in the United States. There, more than two decades later, I picked up a booklet containing a number of pieces by a writer named Elie Wiesel.

At some moments in life one knows one has just been struck by a flash of truth. Everything comes together at that point: something happens, a new insight is born. Such a moment is not easily forgotten. I was aware of my particular moment when I read "Face in the Window," a passage its author called "a legend of our time." With powerful, graphic words it describes a man who watches without comment the deportation of the Jews of his town. He says nothing, he does nothing. He only observes. He is the symbol of a person, a nation, a world's inertia in the face of evil: the "I-don't-want-to-get-involved" syndrome.

The piece touched me deeply. I knew nothing of Elie Wiesel. Not who he was, nor where he came from. But I felt instant kinship with him. He felt what I felt, and he knew how to express the feelings. He had the gift, the power, and the strong urge to make the words come out. And he spoke to me.

I heard Elie Wiesel speak at public lectures. I saw him on television, knew his face from the covers of his many books. He was famous.

When my publisher asked whether I could write a book about Wiesel for young people, I said yes, not because I am an expert on Wiesel, but because we both lived through the same unusual time and he expressed so many feelings which I could share.

On a bright January day, I traveled to New York for my first face-to-face meeting with Elie Wiesel. My appointment with him was in a mid-Manhattan office suite where an organization had lent him space. In a prior telephone conversation, he had given me explicit directions how to reach his office. I was impressed with his concern that I should not get lost.

I was properly nervous for this interview with a celebrity. The dark-eyed slender man in the trim gray business suit welcomed me with a sweet smile and did not act like a celebrity at all. With old-world courtesy he ushered me into the room where we would talk.

We sat in the small office and he spoke to me of his childhood, especially of his parents. I had brought along fragments of my manuscript-to-be, and he was particularly interested in seeing that I had the right "tone" in my opening pages. In his own writing, he told me, he must feel the words "sing" before he is sure he is on the right track and can continue with the story.

Sitting on a hard chair facing me, Wiesel answered my many questions patiently. I had the feeling I had known this man all of my life: I was seeing a friend. I felt united to him by the fact that, as children, our lives were altered by the Holocaust.

After the interview was over, I wandered through the lunch-hour crowd on East 42nd Street. Originally, I had planned to spend the afternoon with friends in New York. Now, I found I no longer wanted to keep the date.

I had just experienced a homecoming. Those who have heard Wiesel speak at an "encounter" know the sensation: it is a feeling of understanding completely, and of being completely understood. For me, it was an experience I needed to hug to myself, to enfold and digest in private, before talking about it and sharing it with others. I took the next train back to Philadelphia.

"Make this book your own," he said to me when shaking my hand in farewell that day. "Tell the story the way you feel it."

My aim is to tell you that story as the journey of a victim traveling through hell and emerging as a victor. Afterwards, I hope, you will turn to the writings of Elie Wiesel and understand just a little more clearly why the things he has to say concern you, too.

Part I

View of the Main Square in Sighet, Elie Wiesel's Hometown

Permission to reproduce stills from the film Sighet, Sighet *courtesy of The Images Film Ar*

The Wiesels' House on Serpent Street in Sighet

Permission to reproduce stills from the film Sighet, Sighet *courtesy of The Images Film A*

1

In a small wooden house facing a narrow, cobblestoned street, a young boy of slender build, with thoughtful brown eyes and dark hair and side-curls, stood at a window, gazing up at the distant Carpathian Mountains which circled his hometown. It was a view to which he awoke every morning of his life, and he never tired of it. This was Sighet, his home, the small valley town in Transylvania, where he, Eliezer—or Leizer, as his family called him—was born on September 30, 1928, as the third child, and only son, of Shlomo and Sarah Wiesel. These same windswept mountains which he glimpsed from his window were once the home of the sainted Israel Baal Shem Tov, Master of the Good Name. Elie liked to believe that from here, too, the Baal Shem's guiding influence had gone out to his followers, the pious men who were called "Hasidim," taking their name from the Hebrew word for "grace" or "piety."

In the Hasidic community of Sighet, innumerable legends and stories were told about the Baal Shem. Some of these legends Elie had learned from his grandfather, others from his teachers in the House of Study.

One of the sayings attributed to the Baal Shem appealed to Elie especially. "God sees, God watches. He is in every life, in every thing. The world hinges on His will. It is He who decides how many times the leaf will turn in the dust before the wind blows it away."

Occasionally, the young boy wondered how so many stories about one person could all be true: at other times he marveled at the power of those legends to survive two centuries and still move and influence people. What was it about those words which transmitted a faith so strong that it literally leaped over the hills Elie saw before him?

Elie frequently asked himself such questions; most of the time he found no answers. Questions concerning religious topics mattered greatly to the people of his town. They were among the favorite subjects discussed and debated in the pulsing, thriving Jewish community of over ten thousand souls, a generous third of Sighet's total population. During Elie's childhood, more Jews lived in Sighet than in any town of comparable size in the whole region.

Sighet was only a small spot on the map of northern Transylvania, in the heart of the Balkans. The tree-covered mountains of Transylvania held treasures of ore and minerals, while its fertile valleys grew large, life-sustaining food crops. Such natural wealth caused neighboring countries to covet the region throughout its history. Always see-sawing between rulers, Transylvania has belonged to them all at one time: to Hungary, Rumania, Austria, the Turkish Empire, Russia, and Germany. When Elie grew up there, the area was under Rumanian rule.

No matter who ruled it, the Jews of Sighet had strong feelings of identification with this region of long, icy winters and short, hot summers. As early as the seventeenth century their forebears had lived there. Merchants and traders, craftsmen and teachers, they had served both their own and the surrounding Christian communities. Like all Jewish communities, Sighet had its ritually approved food supply, its synagogues and Jewish day schools, its Hebrew presses and books, and its own consecrated ground for Jewish burials.

Most of Sighet's Jewish citizens were extremely poor, yet all contributed in their way to the lifestyle of the town. The big weekly event was market day, when everyone with merchandise to sell, be it poultry or candles, shoes or furniture, carried these goods into town on horsedrawn carts, or even on foot. All day the sounds of haggling between merchants and housewives rang stridently through the square as freshness and price of wares were argued.

A single shot of cognac, one glass of steaming tea sustained a man for the length of a whole evening as he read the foreign newspapers and magazines provided for its customers by the local cafe.

In the parlors of houses on Jews' Street, suitable marriages were arranged by mothers of eligible daughters with mothers of sons possessing the right background and age.

In the stuffy, dark study halls of the yeshivot, pious Jewish boys drank in the words of the Talmud from morning to night.

It was this deeply traditional, religious atmosphere which made Sighet special to its townspeople. Whether a man was a bootmaker, storekeeper, baker, or laborer, his life centered around his family, his community, and the Holy Laws. Those who were poor helped the ones who had even less, but all shared one day in the week on which they felt rich. Many years later, such a day—the Sabbath—was described by the hero of one of Elie's books, *The Town Beyond the Wall:*

Up against a range of high, impassable mountains and flanked by two rivers as wide as oceans, Szerencseváros was a small city, happy and poor. Even the rich were poor there, and even the poor were happy. Happiness in Szerencseváros came down to its natural expression: enough bread and wine for the Sabbath meal. So the poor toiled six days by the sweat of their brows, that they might have bread and wine for the seventh.

Like a mantle of purple silk the Sabbath came to drape the city at sundown on Friday. The city's face changed visibly. Merchants closed their shops, coachmen went home because there were no passengers, the pious proceeded to the ritual baths to purify their bodies. The Sabbath is compared to a queen: it is proper to have body and soul clean to merit her visit. The Sabbath: the essence of Judaism. The divine revelation in Time.

Through half-open doors and windows the same song of welcome spread through the deserted streets: "Peace upon you, O angels of peace; peace upon you as you come and peace upon you as you go."

In the Wiesels' corner house on Serpent Street, as in all Jewish homes in Sighet, no work was done during the observance of the Sabbath. By the time sunset came on Friday, all the house-cleaning had been done and enough food had been cooked to last the family for the next twenty-four hours. Since no stranger must go hungry during that time, most housewives prepared sufficient amounts of food for unexpected guests.

The time between sunset Friday and the end of next day's twilight was completely separated from all other days of the week. It was a pause from work, routine, and normal activity. Shabbat was a healing time, a time for love, for peace, for rest. All other days of the week led to it, and from it flowed the inspiration to face the days that came after it. When Elie's mother, dressed in her best clothes, a shawl covering her dark hair, approached the Sabbath candles, it was a sign that the week's work had come to a halt: the Sabbath had entered their home. She lighted two candles. This commemorated the biblical admonition to "remember" and "observe." When the candles were burning, the mother drew her hands around them and toward her face at least three times. By doing this, she symbolized the ushering in of the Sabbath. But she also drew the candles' light and warmth into her soul. Finally, covering her eyes with her hands, Sarah Wiesel blessed the lights: "Blessed are You, Lord our God, King of the Universe, Who has sanctified us with His commandments and commanded us to light the Sabbath candles."

When, as a young child, Elie saw his mother preside over a table of snowy linen and sparkling silver candlesticks, he thought of her as a Sabbath princess, at peace, serene and loving. On the special occasions when his grandfather shared their Sabbath meal and led their singing of the benedictions, he felt that their table was indeed an altar and that the angels must be hovering nearby, just as his grandfather told him they did whenever people observed the Sabbath.

Sarah was a tender and loving mother. Looking down at the dark-eyed baby boy to whom she sang lullabies every night, she must have sometimes wondered what kind of person her only son would become. Would he remember these stories and songs with which she put him to sleep? Had he inherited the gift for storytelling from her own father, Reb Dodye Feig, whose wonderful Hasidic tales she had heard and absorbed in her childhood, and which she was now repeating to this little boy of her own? Sarah liked to think that little Leizer's eyes showed an especially strong interest in the stories she was telling him, as if he understood every word. A baby's mind is so impressionable . . . and it seemed to Sarah that this child was far more interested in listening to her than her two daughters had been at the same age. Would her boy follow in the path of her father, who celebrated his love for God in stories and songs glorifying the Almighty, or would he be like his own father, Shlomo, who believed that nothing was as important as man's love for mankind?

Sarah Wiesel was a highly educated woman. At a time when few Jewish girls pursued an academic education, she had attended and been graduated from high school. In her strict religious home, no German books were allowed, because they were considered too worldly, too removed from pious thought. Yet Sarah loved the German classics, and learned to read and speak German so she could memorize and quote whole sections from the writings of Goethe and Schiller. Her secular knowledge never interfered with her strong religious feelings.

Elie always remembered his mother as being beautiful. Her melodious voice, reassuring and positive, made all his worries disappear. As a young girl, she must have been strikingly attractive. Years later, a family friend told Elie how Sarah had once accompanied her father, Dodye Feig, on a visit into town from their home seven kilometers outside Sighet. Sarah was seated on their horsedrawn wagon as it moved past the spot where a young man named Shlomo Wiesel was standing in the street. Shlomo did not know who she was or where she lived, but she was so beautiful in his eyes that he fell in love with her during that moment. He followed the wagon on foot until it stopped. Then he asked the coachman who the young lady was. Shlomo did not speak to Sarah directly, but shortly afterward, he made a trip to the village where Dodye Feig lived and asked him for the hand of his youngest daughter.

As a married woman and mother Sarah found that the demands on her energy were tiring. She helped her husband in his business, often taking over for him in his absence. She kept house for her growing family, with one servant, Martha, to aid her in running the household. Still, Sarah found time to transmit her own deep religious faith to her children. Elie always felt warmly loved by her. Even when he grew older and Sarah could no longer spend as much time with him as she had done when he was a baby, the love and understanding between them did not change. Elie loved his mother with great intensity. He felt he owed her the life of his soul, that she had given him so much for which he had never thanked her. He took for granted that she knew how much he loved her, yet in later years he often regretted that he had never put it into words. Perhaps, though, he finally did so in his novel *Dawn*, whose hero, Elisha, recalls his mother in the following way:

> I was very fond of my mother. Every evening, until I was nine or ten years old, she put me to sleep with lullabies or stories. There is a goat beside your bed, she used to tell me, a goat of gold. Everywhere you go in life, the goat will guide you and protect you. Even when you are grown up and very rich, when you know everything a man can know and possess all that he should possess, the goat will still be near you.

If Elie, during his early years, felt closer to his mother, it was because Shlomo Wiesel was a very busy man who had little time to spend at home. Shlomo owned a grocery store in the town. More than a food shop, it was stocked with all the wares of a general store and was open for business from early morning until late at night. Reb Shlomo operated the store with the help of his wife and their two older daughters, Bea and Hilda.

Elie remembers his father as being in constant motion,

rushing to or from his store or running to meetings. When he was at home, it was because he was too exhausted to be out. A cultured, educated man, Shlomo Wiesel was deeply involved in civic affairs. He was one of the men on whom the smooth functioning of Sighet's Jewish community depended. He was consulted on all the problems which befell the community council. Whether it was providing a dowry for an orphaned girl, finding medical care for a needy older person, or helping someone to stay out of prison, Shlomo could always be counted on for help.

He was just as respected by the Christian community and had friends among Sighet's business people and local officials, who listened to him, valued his opinions, and aided him when he needed "connections."

"He was an enlightened man who believed in man," Elie was to say of his father in later years.

Only one day each week did Shlomo stop running. Clad in his prayer shawl, his head covered in the presence of God, Reb Shlomo went to synagogue to pray in the tradition of his people. He observed the holidays and kept the Sabbath as the most important holy day of the week. On that day, his store was closed and he prayed at services instead, Elie at his side.

Surrounded by the strong religious beliefs of his wife's side of the family, Shlomo balanced this influence by living his daily life in a rational way. It was the real, the unsentimental that Shlomo could accept. He was a very practical man, who thought it his duty to bring up his only son to respect and trust his fellow-man.

On his Saturdays at home, Shlomo studied and meditated. He was an avid reader with a broad range of interests, from history to psychology, and he insisted that his children, too, become versed in secular subjects. It was his father who made Elie learn the modern Hebrew language and who introduced him to modern Hebrew literature.

As a young child, Elie often felt lonely. It was the loneliness of a small boy whose working parents had to be away from home too much, and whose two older sisters did not share his interests. Elie was not a happy, bubbling child. He was very serious, read constantly, and did not enjoy participating in the more physical games played by some of the other children he knew. Of course, Jewish children did not play outside in the streets of Sighet. The near-poverty of most Jewish families ruled out the possession of toys and games by their children. Elie did love playing chess. He learned the game early and played with his father, when Shlomo had time for him, but also with his own friends, who were equally interested and skilled at chess.

For Elie, life was truly wonderful on those special occasions when his grandfather, a real Hasid, visited town. Dodye Feig was an energetic man with a joyous personality, a celebrity among his own people. He was a follower of the Wishnitz dynasty and had known the founder of that Hasidic sect, which added to his fame. Dodye's exuberance surfaced particularly when he sang Hasidic songs, of which he knew an inordinate number, to Elie's delight, more than were known by most of the pious folk in Sighet. Nothing gray and dismal had a chance when Reb Dodye Feig was around. Nothing lifted his young grandson's spirits higher than the sound of Dodye's horse as it trotted over the cobblestones of their street and came to a halt in front of their house.

Elie always felt completely understood by his grandfather. He could discuss any topic under the sun with him, freely, without hesitation. Best of all, when talking to Dodye, Elie knew he was never looked down upon because he was only a child. His grandfather accepted him as a person, unique and special, and made him feel truly loved. In return, Elie loved Reb Dodye, his mother's father, more than any male in the family.

Dodye's name was actually David. Dodye meant "Little David." It was a term of endearment used by the people who loved him best.

Elie did not see his grandfather nearly as often as he wished. The old man lived some seven kilometers outside of Sighet and came into town only a few times during the year. He usually arrived for the holidays, and then he stayed with his daughter's family, whose home was conveniently located across the street from his favorite sanctuary. When Dodye went there to pray, Elie went with him.

During the rest of the year, Elie attended the larger synagogues in Sighet with his father, but it was the service in the small Hasidic House of Prayer which stirred him. Elie's dark eyes sparkled with Reb Dodye beside him. The pallor of the young boy's pointed face, with its dangling side-curls, contrasted sharply with the ruddy complexion of the white-bearded old man who wore his fur-bordered hat and the good black satin caftan reserved for the High Holy Days. His grandfather gave Elie confidence; he made him feel at home amid the pious, chanting men in their long black coats. In the candlelit room, all were united in kinship, all were part of God in His sanctuary.

Dodye Feig radiated love. Everyone felt his presence with pleasure. When he opened his mouth to sing the glory of God, others turned to listen to him . . . then joined him in singing. Hasidim believed their singing to be a direct channel to God. Their songs expressed what they felt: their joy, their sadness, their love. Their singing was their ladder to heaven. Dodye rocked back and forth when he sang; his body itself became an instrument of prayer. Hearing his grandfather sing roused Elie to a joy he knew only at very special moments. It was like being close to the presence of God.

Occasionally Elie's mother took him to Dodye's home village, where the old man kept a store and operated a small farm, without any outside help. Dodye's neighbors were Christian peasants, to whom he dispensed friendly advice and help when they came to him for their wares. For Elie, the few short hours with his grandfather were always over too soon. When it came time to say goodbye, inevitably tears ran down his face at the moment of separation, even when Dodye told him: "Look at me and you will not cry."

2

ELIE WAS VERY UNHAPPY when he was sent to school for the first time. Just three years old, he was upset at this first real separation from his mother and invented a new illness every day so he might stay home with her a little longer. He sat on the small wooden bench in a dark room of the *cheder*, the traditional Jewish primary school and, along with other neighborhood children, learned the letters of the Hebrew alphabet. His teacher was an old man, hired by the community to instruct the very young in this basic step of their education. Elie was not alone in his unhappiness: most of the children in his class expressed rebellion. But for him, the fear and pain of separation were acute. He distrusted the school, the teacher, and the words he was supposed to learn; all of them, he felt, were responsible for his eviction from home into the outside world.

He never forgot his initiation into the world of letters, nor the old man, remembered only as the "Betizer Rebbe," who tried gently but firmly to teach the children. Aleph, bet, gimel—these were the keys, the first of twenty-two such keys, with which they would unlock the treasure of knowledge. Elie listened to him carefully, for to the white-bearded, portly teacher these letters were apparently very important. Painstakingly, the children copied the letters into a notebook, writing the Hebrew symbols from right to left. They were mindful that each

14

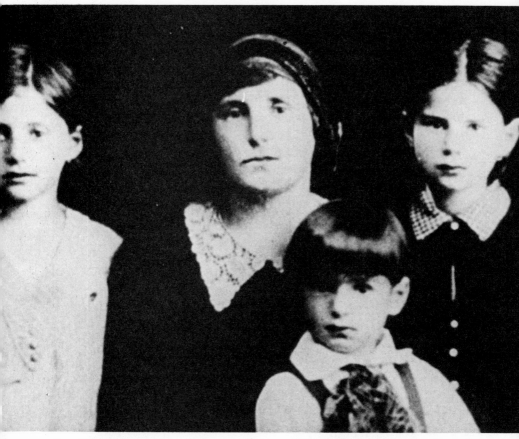

Sarah Wiesel with Her Older Daughters, Hilda and Bea, and Son Elie As a Young Boy

Permission to reproduce stills from the film Sighet, Sighet *courtesy of The Images Film Archive*

Elie Wiesel with His Mother and Younger Sister, Tzipora

Permission to reproduce stills from the film Sighet, Sighet *courtesy of The Images Film Archive*

character, every one a consonant, had various shades of meaning which changed with the position of the letter and with the number of dots in the vowel printed beneath it. The treasure of those twenty-two keys served Elie well; he remembered and used them throughout his life.

Elie was seven years old when Tzipora, the baby of the family, was born. As her brother was closest to her in age, she wanted to play with him at every opportunity, looking up to Elie as only a little sister can. His long school days prevented Elie from spending too much time with her. It was also a bit beneath his schoolboy dignity to do so. But he loved the little girl dearly, and delighted in her brightness and daintiness. Sometimes he wished Tzipora were older so he could share more of his thoughts with her. At this stage of his life he was just emerging from young childhood himself and needed a confidante more than he needed a playmate.

Once, when he was in a particularly low mood, Elie left home without telling anyone where he was headed. He walked for many hours until he reached the countryside where his grandfather lived. Not thinking that he would be missed at home, Elie had felt the urge to see the old man and talk things over with him. Surprised to see him, Reb Dodye did not scold his grandson for this escapade. He made certain that Elie's parents knew where the boy was, sending word with the next coachman traveling to Sighet. Then he sat down to have supper with Elie. When they were finished with their after-meal prayer, Dodye settled down for an evening's conversation.

"Now, tell me," he asked, "what is wrong?"

"Nothing, grandfather. I just missed you very much."

"Is everything all right at home?" The kind eyes looked at him sharply. "No arguments with your parents? Trouble at school?"

"No, grandfather. I wanted to see you."

"I am glad to hear that, my boy. I must confess that in my youth I too ran away a time or two when I had things on my mind. *I* used to go to my rebbe and tell him when things troubled me."

That evening Elie heard some stories from Dodye's own childhood that he had not known. Dodye spoke to him of *his* own father, who at the age of seventy had wanted to learn to play the violin and taken nightly lessons from a gypsy until he could entertain the members of his family with gypsy airs and Hasidic music on Saturday nights. When he was near ninety and felt that he might die soon, Dodye's father had requested that his violin be buried with him. This was just in case the powers in heaven were angry with him, Dodye said; his father could change their mood with his playing.

Elie always remembered the day when he had run away, and in years to come, he never forgot that Dodye was "always ready to help without passing judgment." The stories Dodye told him became his favorites and lasted through a lifetime, but Elie liked it best when his grandfather sang. The melodies were either joyous or sad, but always filled with meaning. In them Elie sensed the agitation and joy, the sorrows and sadness of being a Jew. The songs spoke of the Jew's savage love of justice, and the desire to be one with his God. When he was a child, Elie only knew they were beautiful; later he understood that with his songs his grandfather had passed on to him the tradition of his ancestors.

As his learning progressed, Elie went on to the next teacher. "Zeide the Melamed" taught Bible in a dark, ramshackle two-room house at the end of a court. The house's shabby appearance seemed the proper setting for the teacher, who hit his pupils when they were tardy or did poor work. The children thought him cruel; he flew into rages at their slightest misbehavior. He was a deformed, ugly man who hid his insecurities in temper tantrums. On the straight, hard benches of Zeide's room, the boys spent the endless hours from dawn to darkness facing their teacher, learning and reciting the 613 commandments in the Torah. These *mitzvot* had guided the daily lives of observant Jews for centuries and, in the opinion of their teachers and elders, were still the basis of learning. The voices of the students, chanting in unison, could be heard outside in the passage of the court throughout the six days of the school week. Elie stayed with Zeide for two years.

When Itzhak, the melamed's assistant, taught the local boys next, Elie received an introduction to the Oral Tradition. All the rules of conduct which had developed after the writing of the Torah (the Five Books of Moses) were to be found in the Mishna and the Gemara. In the Mishna all the laws were categorized neatly into sections, such as Family Life, Holy Matters, and Damages, among others, while the Gemara was a book of commentaries dealing with the topics listed in the Mishna. Studying the Oral Tradition gave one an insight into the rules by which the Jewish people lived with each other, with their neighbors, in their universe. The first topic Elie examined under Itzhak's direction dealt with the problem of two people who both claimed ownership of a garment they had found, and their argument over who might rightfully keep it.

At the age of ten, Elie became a student of the "Selishter Rebbe," a man remembered by his pupils for his hard slaps and "a raucous, brutal voice." Those of his students who talked or daydreamed in his class had every reason to regret it. If the warmth of the schoolroom's stove lulled them into sleepiness, or the early winter twilight caused them to yawn, the "wild eyes" of their teacher were sure to fall on them. The strength of his arm on the unsuspecting victim was enough to shake the student's cap off his head and bring him back to the present immediately. Even more frightening than the physical blows was the teacher's behavior during the evening services when he read passages about the Last Judgment to his students. The unhappy man burst into fits of sobbing during these readings, baffling and disturbing the boys in the eerie hours between late afternoon and full darkness.

Elie's later teachers were more normal and considerate of their students. Elie became mature enough to tackle more difficult projects in his talmudic studies; he learned how to untangle sections of a tractate by himself and discovered that there was great satisfaction in finding the clear, precise thought at the heart of a talmudic passage. Despite the long days from six o'clock in the morning until past midnight, Elie was happy in this world of prayer and study.

"I believed profoundly," he says of that time, during which he thought his future life would be devoted to religion. He would become a rabbi; certainly this was what his mother and grandfather would have liked him to become. Better yet, his mother would have liked to see him become both a rabbi and a secular scholar. But there were times when Elie thought he might like to be a maggid best of all.

A maggid was an itinerant preacher who traveled from town to town, giving sermons in the local synagogue on Saturday afternoons. Frequently a maggid came to preach in Sighet. Storytelling was the particular expression of a maggid's teaching. Each colorful story held a lesson which stirred the listeners' emotions, comforting some, scolding others.

Since public entertainment was limited in a small town, especially within a religious community, the visit of a maggid was always an important event. Elie ran to hear each maggid who came to Sighet. Lost in the big crowd which filled the synagogue on such an occasion, the awed young boy listened intently as the maggid held the hushed audience spellbound despite the hard benches. To have such talent and magnetism was God-given, he felt.

Elie was so drawn to legends and mysteries that now even the study of Talmud was no longer enough for him. He wanted to know more. He wanted to find the hidden meanings which eluded him, the answers to questions ancient scholars had already sought: When would the persecution and suffering stop? When would peace come to the whole world? When would the Messiah appear to proclaim the kingdom of God?

In 1941, when he was twelve years old, Elie asked his father to find him a Master who would instruct him in the Kabbala, the teachings and lore of Jewish mysticism. With that key he would then be able to interpret the meanings and mysteries supposedly hidden behind every letter and word of the Bible.

Shlomo Wiesel was not too surprised at Elie's request. He had always been proud of the boy's devotion to his studies. Even when he had needed more help in the family store, he had always insisted that Elie's place be at school instead. Shlomo wanted Elie to become a well-rounded person; the only way to do that was to spend some time every day on Latin, mathematics, and physics. Even the violin lessons Elie took three times a week from the friendly police officer at the station house across the street were part of the plan to give him a general education.

"You are too young to study mysticism," Shlomo told Elie. "You know that a student of the Kabbala should be an older person than you are. Besides, I know of no one in Sighet who could teach you. There are no kabbalists here."

Perhaps Shlomo was a little frightened by the intensity of his son, who spent so much time with his books and ran to the synagogue every evening, where he stayed long after services ended.

Elie was a boy who sought the spirit of the Jewish past in the ghostly atmosphere of half-dark buildings. His father thought Elie's quest into the world of Jewish mysticism might be due to his approaching adolescence. Youngsters developed such strange yearnings during those years. The boy's easy melancholia, his obsession with prayer and with questions regarding the existence of God, were, in the view of his father, possibly a manifestation of his age.

Elie was pale and thin, and he had frequent headaches. Both Shlomo and Sarah worried over him. They consulted all the town doctors on the boy's weight loss and his constant illnesses. They were concerned that Elie ate so very little at the family dinner table. They did not know that twice a week—on Mondays and Thursdays—Elie fasted secretly. It was his hope that self-denial might bring him closer to the religious discipline he wished to attain.

Elie's father had told him that no one in town could teach him the mysteries of the Kabbala, but Elie found his own teacher. His name was Moshe, and he was the caretaker at the synagogue to which Elie went after school hours. Elie had long talks with Moshe, often lasting until the late hours of the night. He felt completely understood by Moshe and spoke to him with emotion about all the topics which troubled him in his relation to the universe.

It was to Moshe that Elie turned, and it was Moshe who read with him in the Zohar—the Book of Splendor—the most important part of the study of the Kabbala.

They read together for hours, the awkward, withdrawn synagogue beadle and the avid young boy, poring over passage after passage, sometimes concentrating on one section until they felt they had truly reached the intended meaning of the words.

During the time Moshe was his Master, Elie felt happy. He loved their discussions, the talks they had about God, about man, about the dialogue between them. Apart from his grandfather, with whom he could talk about everything, Moshe was Elie's first real friend. Certainly he was the first human adult who took the shy boy seriously and treated him as an equal.

When he was thirteen, Elie became a Bar Mitzvah. According to Jewish tradition, he was now an adult and responsible for his actions. Now, on any Sabbath, when the holy Torah scrolls in their beautiful embroidered mantles were removed from the ark and unrolled on the reading lectern, he might be called up to the *bima* to read. From his parents Elie received a handsome gold watch, the customary gift for the important occasion on which a boy turns into a young man. He was also given his first pair of tefillin, the two small leather cases which a devout Jew binds to his forehead and his left arm during his morning prayers. In the Hasidic synagogue of Dodye Feig's favorite rabbi, where Elie's Bar Mitzvah services were held, Elie was honored by having the rabbi himself help him put on the phylacteries for the first time. After that, he used them to start his every weekday, aware of the holy law inscribed on small strips of parchment inside the leather cases: "And these words which I command you this day shall be upon your heart: And you shall teach them diligently to your children, and shall speak of them when you sit in your house, when you walk along the way and when you rise up. You shall bind them for a sign upon your hand, and they shall be as frontlets between your eyes."

Amid the shadows cast by flickering candles, Elie continued his nightly vigils with Moshe. The Book of Splendor was beginning to open up its mysteries to him. He understood meanings he had never realized before. He became aware of the presence of God in everything, good or evil. His own actions and the actions of other people revealed to Elie that everything had its order in the universe. Every human being had inside of him a spark of the divine. That spark yearned to be united with God, who had given it light and life. Every person could reach the presence of God through devotion to the Holy One, observance of His commandments, and the practice of kindness and love for all living things.

Elie was filled with happiness that he was, at last, beginning to acquire some of the meaning for which he had been searching. He lived his days and nights so wrapped up in his inner life that little reached him concerning the events which had been happening on the other side of the mountains.

3

THE FIRST TIME Elie had heard his mother suggest they leave Sighet was on a Shabbat night. The family was still sitting at the table, after the Friday evening meal had been eaten and all the dishes cleared away. When they sang the after-dinner blessings, Sarah did not join in. Instead, she sat very quietly at the table, a faraway look on her face. Elie knew that his mother occasionally mentioned having premonitions of events to come, but it seemed to him that she had looked worried lately. It had been many months since he had seen her relaxed and carefree. And she had been gazing at him in a strange way whenever she thought he didn't notice.

"Why don't we just pack up our belongings, sell the business, and go to Palestine," Sarah burst out suddenly, just as everybody was ready to get up from the table.

"When do you suggest we leave?" Shlomo asked. His tone indicated that he was not taking his wife's suggestion seriously.

"The faster the better. Nothing has been going right for some time and things are not likely to improve. Perhaps we should try to get out while there is still a chance."

At his age, Elie was not especially interested in political matters, and few of the adults outside of his family with whom he had daily contact knew much more than he did. Lately, though, the friends who visited the Wiesel home always had bad news to talk about. Ever since the

23

Germans had marched into Poland in September 1939, many upsetting rumors had been reaching Sighet.

Germany had signed a friendship pact with Russia, then had invaded Poland. This was the start of the Second World War, and it had caught the Jews of Poland in a squeeze between Germany and Russia. As one European country after another capitulated rapidly before the German might, millions of Jews were trapped in the net of Nazi-occupied lands. Reports of killings drifted back to Sighet from Poland; disquietening news from Galicia told of Jews being murdered there. Since France had surrendered in the summer of 1940, Britain alone was trying to hold back Hitler's advancing troops from swallowing all of Europe.

Sighet, too, had known some changes. In August of 1940, due to German pressure, Rumania had been forced to cede the northern part of Transylvania, in which Sighet was situated, to Hungary, a partner in the Germany-Italy-Japan "Axis." This brought the Jewish citizens of Sighet much closer to being under Nazi control, but most of them wanted to believe that the mountain passes, which in winter made travel in and out of their area so difficult, would also keep them out of the reach of the enemy.

Already, though, the spirit of hate that was enveloping all the German-dominated areas of Europe was coming closer to home. The newspapers and radio, with increasing frequency, began expressing anti-Semitic ideas. Their Gentile neighbors, too, now often made anti-Semitic remarks. Elie and his friends knew that Jewish boys in the public schools were often beaten up by other students these days, and that the teachers made a deliberate point of ignoring such attacks.

"This kind of thing has been going on for centuries," Shlomo said, whenever someone remarked to him that times were getting worse. "But it will also straighten out and get better again."

Occasionally Elie caught a strange look on his mother's face when she glanced at his father. "Have you forgotten?" her eyes seemed to ask. And then Elie knew she was thinking of his father's recent prolonged absence from home, and the reason for it. Sighet, being close to the border, had been the destination of many Polish Jews who had tried to flee the Germans since the occupation. If the Hungarian police caught them in Sighet, they were returned to Poland and certain death. Shlomo had an acquaintance on the police force through whom he discovered an unusual regulation which could help these prisoners. Anyone who was arrested carrying foreign money, such as American dollars or British pounds, on his person, was not returned to Poland, but was sent to prison in Budapest, the Hungarian capital, instead. So Shlomo made it his business to obtain as much foreign money as he could. With this, he visited immediately any fleeing Jew who had been arrested by the Sighet police. Thanks to Shlomo's efficiency and the help of several other men who assisted him in this scheme, several hundred Polish refugees had already been saved from the hands of the Germans. One day, however, Shlomo himself was arrested: one of the prisoners had revealed his name under torture.

Shlomo was kept in jail for almost two months. Sarah and her two daughters ran the business, wondering all the while what would happen to him. When Shlomo returned, tired, pale, but tight-lipped about his experience with interrogation and torture, he went back to work . . . and back to helping people escape from Poland.

Shlomo believed in the goodness of men. When his wife argued with him, he told her he was certain their family would be safe. Weren't they important citizens of their hometown? Hadn't the family roots been in Sighet for over three centuries? Who would want to do them any harm? Why, then, leave their home, their friends, their possessions, without being forced to?

All around them, the people the Wiesels knew lived their daily lives, worked at their jobs, spoke with their neighbors. Although there was now a death penalty for those who were caught listening to their shortwave radios, people still tuned in on the news reports from London. Few of them felt personally endangered; few attempted to leave for Palestine or America.

Sarah, however, saw signs which to her boded no good. Now that Sighet was under Hungarian jurisdiction, all Jews were required to register with the police and be classified as Jews. More and more restrictions were being placed on them. In addition, Hungary, too, had entered the war, having joined Germany in attacking Russia in June of 1941. Soon there were food shortages; some foods were rationed or not available at all. As they stood in queues waiting for their rations, some of the townswomen grumbled that it was the Jews who caused the shortages by hoarding everything. Sarah did not like what she saw and heard. Her face kept its worried look.

Deep in Sarah's heart, hidden away from her immediate family, lingered the memory of an experience. She never spoke of it to Shlomo or to her daughters; she had no wish to alarm them, so she kept her fears to herself. But often her thoughts returned to the incident, which had left her uneasy and melancholy.

Every year, just before the High Holy Days, the Rebbe of Wishnitz paid a visit to the faithful of Sighet. He was a Tzaddik, a wise and righteous leader, and his visit was always a major event: from all directions the devout Hasidim of the area streamed into Sighet for the chance of an audience with him. Sarah always went to see the Rebbe when he was in town, taking Elie with her so that he might receive the sage's blessing. She hoped that the exposure to the holy man would influence her boy to grow up and become the kind of Jew who, like her, feared God and loved His commandments.

Hundreds of visitors swarmed near the quarters of the Rebbe, awaiting their turn to see him. Outside his private chamber, at a little table, the Rebbe's scribe wrote out the questions which each visitor hoped to ask the sage of Wishnitz during his meeting with him. Sarah Wiesel, unlike most of those seeking an interview, knew how to read and write. She never used the scribe's services, instead writing out her own *kvittl*, but she always paid the scribe his customary fee, for she knew that his livelihood depended on it and did not wish to deprive him.

Elie was about eight years old at the time of the Rebbe's last visit to Sighet. Holding her boy by the hand, Sarah had entered the private chamber and presented her slip of paper which asked the holy man to tell her something of her son's future.

The Rebbe knew Dodye Feig well and held him in high esteem. He had seen Sarah grow up, and he was also very fond of Elie. That day, he had pulled the little boy up on his knees and had teased him in a friendly fashion, asking him many questions about his studies. To the Rebbe's noticeable pleasure, Elie had answered all the inquiries in great detail. Suddenly, the kind, gray-bearded man turned to Sarah and asked her to leave them alone together for a while.

She had waited outside while Elie was still in the Rebbe's chamber. After about a half-hour, she was allowed to return. This time, in turn, Elie was sent out to wait amid the crowd of chattering, praying, fidgeting Hasidim.

Inside, meanwhile, the holy man revealed a strange prophecy to Sarah. When she emerged from her audience with the sage and walked out into the anteroom, Sarah had been sobbing. Her tears, lasting all the way home, and recurring many times in the weeks to follow, had alarmed Elie, she knew. He had worried greatly about her crying. Often, the little boy asked her whether he had said or done anything wrong during the visit, whether it was his fault that she cried so much. Sarah had assured him that he was not the cause of her tears, but she had never answered his many questions. Almost against her will, she often found herself gazing at the boy, wishing she could see into the future, and yet dreading it. She wondered just what the Rebbe had meant, and how to interpret what he had said.

That was to be the holy man's last visit to Sighet. Political events and travel restrictions stopped him from moving about. Sarah never unsealed the Rebbe's strange prophecy regarding her son.

A very young person often lives in a world of his own. His personal problems appear more important to him than those of others. Elie heard the arguments between his parents: his mother's urgings for, his father's reasonings against, leaving their home. Certainly he heard enough bits of daily conversation swirling around him to know that the Jews of Sighet were deeply troubled. But at the age of thirteen, Elie and his friends—Haimi Kahan, Itzu Goldblat, and Yerachmiel Mermelstein—shared school, synagogue, and the fervent time of adolescence.

Elie's goal was the pursuit of truth. His inner life admitted only ingredients necessary to that goal. His strange yearning for the spiritual, which his father considered a symptom of adolescence, took more eccentric turns. Now study and fasting were no longer enough: to be closer to God, one had to be pure. Elie and his friends visited the *mikveh,* the ritual bath, before every prayer service.

Finally, even the age of rebellion became wrapped in a religious whirl. Following a custom which held that young people should have a synagogue, even a school, of their own, since they were different from adults and perhaps misunderstood by their elders, Elie and his friends decided they wanted to study and pray without community interference.

Haimi Kahan's father, an eminent scholar, took it upon himself to aid the enterprising youngsters. Every morning at six o'clock, in a room specifically their own, the learned man met with his son and the boy's friends and led them in talmudic studies. In their new, isolated private world, the boys felt very secure. The lessons they learned here, the prayers they recited, were their safety-wrap. It would surely protect them from harm if the events of the outside world ever reached into their lives.

4

NEW EDICTS. New restrictions. Hungarian
Jews lost their citizenship; their registration papers pro-
claimed them to be stateless. Anyone who did not possess
the proper registration was considered a foreigner.

Elie stood on the platform of Sighet's railroad station,
saying a silent goodbye to his first adult best friend.
Moshe, the caretaker of the synagogue, was among the
"foreign" Jews being deported from the town by the
Hungarian police. The order had come suddenly,
abruptly: all foreign Jews had to leave. The order was
carried out immediately.

It was not a private parting. Elie, clutching his books in
a satchel, shared the narrow platform with as many
members of the Jewish community as found room to stand
on the walkway at the early morning hour. With long,
somber faces they watched, having brought food packages
for the deportees. The onlookers had tears running down
their cheeks, responding to the wild weeping of the group
huddled near the tracks, under the revolvers and clubs of
the police.

In the sooty dawn, Elie's tears blurred his vision. All
the faces around him merged into one anonymous crowd.
Shoulders hunched forward, his dark eyes burning, Elie's
white face strained for a look at Moshe. Already, his friend
and teacher, the man who had shared some of his

innermost thoughts, had become a stranger. He was a part of the gray mass pushed and herded by the police toward the lined-up boxcars. Elie winced at the sight of Moshe, bent over and timid, moving as if in a trance toward the wide opening at the center of the freight car. Just before he disappeared into the car, Moshe tried to look around. "Perhaps he is looking for me," Elie thought. He saw his teacher attempt to raise his arm, but he understood that Moshe really could not wave. There was no room for Moshe to move his body and his arms were burdened with a parcel of food. Soon he was swallowed altogether, a single drop in a puddle of water.

He was gone. The man who had opened to him some of the secrets in the great books, who had helped him interpret important wisdom . . . this man was helpless to do anything about his own fate. He was a mere toy against the brute force of the Hungarian policemen, who now slammed down the doors of the boxcars and sealed them shut. Within moments the train moved out of the station. Soon it disappeared from view.

Amid sighs and murmurs, the people on the platform moved away, their tears drying. Behind him Elie heard a man mutter that it was wartime, after all, so perhaps it was not too surprising that something like this had to happen. Elie ached far too much to question why adults accepted surprises so readily. Did anyone in this large crowd, now thinning out into the street, feel as sad as he did?

He had said goodbye to a friend, and Elie hated goodbyes. This time it was more than leaving his beloved grandfather behind on the farm after visiting there. As Elie lifted his school bag and settled it on his back, he wondered how the Jews of Sighet could walk away from the station and return to their houses, to their stores, to their studies, as if nothing had happened.

Elie, too, went back to his studies. He was deeply immersed in the talmudic tractate taught by Reb Nochem Hersh, father of his friend, Haimi. Reb Hersh was a good teacher; studying with him was illuminating. The talmudic sages' statement: "Whosoever occupies himself with Torah, keeps suffering at a distance," lulled Elie and his fellow students into a feeling of timelessness and safety. They sat at their early-morning studies; they prayed before and after reading the Talmud. So wrapped up were they in their mantle of learning and faith that it was hard for this small band of friends to believe that any evil from the outside world could harm them.

Still, there were times when Elie, while poring over lines of Hebrew script in the heavy books before him, found his thoughts drifting. He thought of Moshe. Where was his friend now? What had happened to the gentle beadle, and to the others, whom the train had carried away?

It was worse in the evenings. When late services were over and the pious old men had drifted out of the synagogue on their way home, Elie missed Moshe most. It was then, after the voices were hushed and the lights extinguished, that he and Moshe had studied together, a single candle glimmering near them. Elie missed their talks. Reading in the Book of Splendor was not a project for one. You needed a guide, someone to share the discoveries.

Though Elie was a religious-school student, the law demanded that he also fulfill the educational requirements in effect in the state schools. As soon as he reached high school age, Shlomo registered him as a student at the regional high school located in the Hungarian town of Debreczin. Once a year Elie rode the train to Debreczin and sat for the examination which would advance him to the next grade. During the month preceding the yearly trip, he studied especially hard to make up for the other eleven months when he concentrated on his religious learning. One of the secular-school requirements on which he was tested was Latin.

Fortunately for Elie, and for some of his friends, a lady living in Sighet was qualified to teach Latin. Elie went to her house every week, loaded down with books, note-books, and a carefully wrapped parcel. The books and notebooks were devoted to the study of Latin. The parcel contained Elie's highly treasured phonograph records. For the trip to the teacher's house was sweetened by the reward which followed the declensions and conjugations: the teacher owned a record-player, one of the very few in Sighet, and she allowed Elie to use it as a bonus for work done well.

The love of music came to Elie naturally. It was transmitted through the Hasidic melodies he heard at the Sabbath table, through an appreciation of his mother's lovely, clear soprano when she sang the *lieder* she cherished, through his father, who loved synagogue liturgy. Elie had little knowledge of classical music. One day he heard his first recording, the voice of the world-famous cantor Yossele Rosenblatt, and the sensation of so much beauty was almost akin to pain. A feeling of exaltation came over Elie. He became aware that the human voice, performing in sounds glorifying God, was the highest expression of prayer. With the introduction to such sounds, another dimension was added to Elie's life. He became an ardent music lover. Every groshen which came his way was saved for eventual investment in another wax disk to be added to his record collection. The brilliant voices of the famous cantors of his day— Rosenblatt, Kwartin, Sirota—brought intense pleasure to the young boy, who listened raptly as the sounds emerged from the horn of the gramophone in his teacher's living room.

Every Saturday afternoon, some of the pious youngsters of Sighet gathered to partake of the third meal at the small synagogue where Elie liked to go. When the eating and the singing were done, the last meal of the Sabbath ended with discussions and study of religious topics. Elie looked forward to the times when his friend Yerachmiel Mermelstein came to the synagogue to speak to the young people about Palestine.

Yerachmiel was different. As good a talmudic scholar as any of Elie's contemporaries, Yerachmiel had a firm footing in current events. His great interest lay in the political status of the Land of Israel.

"Someday there will be a new Jewish state. Even now, fellow-Jews are living in Palestine and arming for the day when they will overthrow the British and free our land," he told his listeners wherever he went.

Yerachmiel's heart was inflamed with the idea that he might someday live in Palestine. And he made it his mission to tell everyone he could about that future.

"Every one of us can make this state a reality. I am collecting money for the Jewish National Fund. With that, we can purchase land, pieces of land on which our people, from everywhere, will live one day."

Elie was most impressed with the visions of the Holy Land Yerachmiel opened to him. When his friend spoke before people, he was a different person. He was so excited that his voice shook, but everyone could see how he burned with the desire to share his message. Yerachmiel's talks were eye-openers: Elie had never thought one could get to the Holy Land without fasting and praying. His friend said that it was possible to fight for Palestine, that one could actually go there to live. To show everyone how serious he was about his goal, Yerachmiel pulled out a small, well-worn book that he always carried in his pocket. He showed it to the boys, who listened to him intently.

A book of modern Hebrew grammar. That was one of the first steps they must take. Otherwise, how would they be able to understand anyone who spoke Ivrit, the language of modern Palestine? This was a topic already familiar to Elie. Hadn't his father mentioned to him many times that he should learn modern Hebrew? Here, at least, was something his father and his friend had in common.

"Lend me your Hebrew grammar book," he begged Yerachmiel, promising that he would guard his friend's prized possession with the utmost care. In true friendship, Yerachmiel agreed to a week's loan.

5

ONE EVENING, many months later, Elie walked into his synagogue for maariv prayers. Huddled on a bench near the rear, a familiar figure caught his eye: Moshe was back. Moshe back in Sighet? Elie was so surprised, so happy to see him, he could hardly wait for the short service to be over, so he could talk to his friend.

Something had happened to Moshe. Sitting with him, trying to speak with him, Elie could not understand why Moshe was so different. He looked in vain for the friend and tutor he had known during their earlier conversations. Gone was the timid, retiring person with whom he had sat night after night, who had explained so patiently the meaning of each letter in the Zohar. The Moshe who had returned in his place was a wild, driven human being who talked incessantly. Pulling people by the sleeve, he earnestly harangued everyone he saw to listen to his tale. Eyes rolling, arms flying, he spoke to anyone who would listen about the events which had befallen him and his fellow-deportees from Sighet.

"Listen to me," he begged. He told about the cattle cars that had carried them away into Poland, where their Hungarian police guards were replaced by German troops. The soldiers unloaded the Jews from the train and marched them off into a forest. There, the people were instructed to dig deep ditches.

36

"Listen," he pleaded, describing how the deportees were forced to stand beside the finished ditches, how the German soldiers had raised their machine guns and fired into the group. One by one, men, women, and children had fallen, until not one of Moshe's companions was left standing . . .

Moshe had never sought out people before. Now, after his return to Sighet, he visited every house. Every Jewish family in town heard his story. Wild-eyed, he told them how he alone had escaped, receiving only a leg wound, but feigning death, while the bodies of the others fell on him and covered him. How the Germans, their work finally done, had left the Galician forest scene . . .

Moshe repeated his story wherever someone would listen to him. Day after day, he spoke of the horrors that had befallen him. Soon the people of Sighet grew tired of his tales. His stories made them very uncomfortable; it was easier to doubt him than to believe him.

Elie again sat with his friend in the synagogue every night, just as he had so fervently wished he might during Moshe's absence. But even he wondered about Moshe's behavior. He began to pity him. Everything was so different; his friend acted in a bizarre fashion. Moshe was grief-stricken over the lack of reaction his message received. His warning had reached ears unwilling to listen. He was not taken seriously by those who heard his story.

"You don't understand," he said in despair. "You can't understand. I have been saved miraculously. I managed to get back here. Where did I get the strength from? I wanted to come back to Sighet to tell you the story of my death. So that you could prepare yourselves while there was still time. To live? I don't attach any importance to my life any more. I'm alone. No, I wanted to come back, and

to warn you. And see how it is, no one will listen to
me. . . ."

(Night)

That night, after speaking to Moshe, Elie lay awake in his
bed long after the rest of the family had fallen asleep.
Only Tzipora's rhythmic breathing reached his corner of
the room they shared; no other sound disturbed the
silence of the house. Moshe's grief had touched Elie, and
now he was worried. Why had the deportees from Sighet
been killed? Why did everyone he knew act as if it hadn't
really happened? Couldn't the same fate befall them, Elie
and his family? He felt sorry for Moshe. In the dark,
frightening thoughts filled Elie's mind and kept him from
sleeping.

Elie waited for Shlomo's return the following evening.
He sat patiently while his father ate his late supper,
noticing how Shlomo looked ever more tired these days.
Everything about him appeared gray and weary. Elie
gathered courage; he didn't want to hurt his father's
feelings.

"Father, why don't we pack up and leave for Palestine?"

This was the first time Elie had taken up the subject,
but he had heard his mother mention it several times
lately. As a child, he had not dared to make such a
suggestion before. Moshe's story and Yerachmiel's ardent
description of Palestine had been working on him, and he
now felt it his duty to speak out.

"Why?"

Elie did not want his father to think he was afraid or
that he had been listening to too many rumors.

"I think every Jewish person always dreams of living in
Palestine," he answered. "I think about it often."

"Son, at my age it is too late to start over again in

another place, another country. But if you want to go to Palestine, you may go."

"Alone?"

Shlomo nodded his head. His father was not being unkind, but Elie sensed that the answer would not change. He had gotten no further than his mother. Neither one of them could convince Shlomo that the Wiesels should leave Sighet.

Rosh Hashana 1943. The sharp blast of the ram's horn—the shofar—began the most important week in the Jewish religious calendar. It was the start of the Ten Days of Awe. Elie, like everyone else, was acutely aware of his sins as he sought forgiveness on this Day of Judgment. The prayers meant even more to Elie now because this was the first High Holy Day on which he was allowed to pray as an adult. Like his grandfather, like the Hasidim near him, he wore his *talith* over his shoulders with pride. Now that he was past the age of Bar Mitzvah, it was his privilege to pray as a member of the adult religious community. He implored God to set him on the right path for a better year ahead—a year of life which, he prayed, would be granted to him, to his parents, to his three sisters, to his grandmother, and to his grandfather, who stood beside him.

Elie took his praying seriously. He prayed not only for his own family, but asked God to watch over the whole world. He was certain that a personal link existed between himself and God, that God would grant his requests, those he made for himself and those made on behalf of others. Elie believed this with all his heart. In these moments of intense communication with God, Elie was convinced that his prayers could bring the Messiah into the world. The Redeemer, who would bring salvation to the Jewish people, and peace and justice to all mankind, could only be brought by man. But God would appoint that individual as His messenger. Elie, who felt such love for his religion, and for his fellow-Jews, was certain that God knew of it, and would, at the appointed time, make use of him.

Services in the House of Prayer ended long after darkness had fallen. Old friends flocked around Dodye Feig, wishing him and Elie a *shana tova*, a good year. No one lingered long that evening; everyone wanted to be at home with his family.

Outside, the street lamps were lit. A Hungarian gendarme on duty outside the police station on the corner disdainfully watched the crowd of dark-clad, bearded men dispersing in the direction of their homes.

The eyes of Dodye Feig twinkled with happiness and anticipation as he and Elie crossed the street, headed for the brightly lit Wiesel home, where a special holiday meal awaited them.

Rosh Hashana. In every household, the Jews of Sighet wished one another a good New Year, hoping it would indeed turn out to be one.

6

THE COMING OF spring 1944 found thoughts of war on nearly everyone's mind. In Sighet, whether meeting by chance in the marketplace, visiting each other's homes, or attending sessions of the community council, Jews discussed the progress of the war. No one knew what to believe. When they listened to the forbidden BBC broadcasts from London, people learned that the fighting was not going well for Germany: the Russian armies were pursuing the retreating Germans. That was good news. The events described by Radio Budapest were far more worrisome: on March 19, 1944, Germany had occupied all of Hungary.

From a visitor who had been to Budapest and spoken to many people there, the Wiesels learned the details. Hitler had been furious with the Hungarian Regent, Miklós Horthy, for not cooperating fully with the German war effort. The Regent and the members of his cabinet had been summoned to a meeting with Hitler. While they were away, German troops had marched into Hungary. In the aftermath, all labor unions were dissolved; there were no more political parties. The only newspapers permitted to appear were the official organs of the new fascist government.

The same visitor reported that the Jews who lived in Budapest feared to go out into the streets. Hungarian National Socialists and the dreaded gangs of the Fascist

41

Arrow Cross were breaking into synagogues. There were daily attacks on Jewish shops and businesses; Jews were beaten in public places. People in Sighet, hearing the visitor's information, shook their heads in dismay. They were thankful that Budapest was so many miles away.

In his house, Elie watched as his mother, like other Jewish housewives in Sighet, got ready for Passover 1944. She removed and cleaned out all traces of bread and flour from her kitchen, preparing for the week-long observance during which only matzos, unleavened bread, could be eaten, a reminder of the Exodus from Egypt when the Israelites could not finish baking their bread before fleeing their homes. Elie's older sisters helped their mother put away the daily china. From an out-of-the-way cupboard, they brought out the special set of dishes used only during Passover. The chatter and giggles which were the usual accompaniments to these preparations were subdued. The hustle and movement of making the knaidlach for the soup and baking the potato kugels for the Seder meal were not present this year. Apprehension hung over everyone.

For some days, German army cars had been patrolling the streets of Sighet. Most of the town's citizens tried to keep out of sight. From behind their window curtains they peeked at the black uniforms and steel helmets of the feared German soldiers and recognized that their insignia—the death's head—was not that of the regular army but belonged to the special troops of the Waffen-SS. Shivers ran down the back of every Jew who glimpsed it.

Elie was especially disappointed that Dodye Feig would not be at their Seder. Only the immediate family would be present for the first night's meal. Sarah explained that conditions for travel were not the best, and that was why

Elie's grandfather couldn't come, and why no other guests had been invited.

It had been many weeks since Dodye had come into town to spend Shabbat with them. Elie, who treasured every hour his grandfather spent under their roof, remembered that last weekend with perfect clarity. Dodye had said something unusual to him, just before he had climbed aboard his cart to go home on the Sunday morning of that weekend. Elie knew it was meant just for him, because his grandfather had whispered it into his ear: "You are Jewish, your task is to remain Jewish. The rest is up to God." Elie had not cried on this occasion when his grandfather's horse pulled the cart out of sight. He had wondered what Dodye's words meant. He was still wondering.

At dawn of the last day of Passover came the loud knock on the front door that all had dreaded. The leaders of the Jewish community were arrested and dragged before the SS officers quartered in the town. "From now on, all orders will come from us," the community leaders were informed. "Your lives will depend on your close cooperation with us."

The next blow came immediately. Jews were not to leave their homes for three days—under penalty of death. Elie, pale and frightened, witnessed the invasion of their home by Hungarian policemen conducting house searches for valuables in all Jewish homes on the street. He watched Shlomo silently hand over all precious belongings in the house. Gold, silver, jewelry, money— whatever was found—was taken away. Keeping anything from the police meant death.

Elie worried about his gold watch, which he had hidden carefully amid his schoolbooks. He turned cold when one of the policemen pointed to the children's room. "Anything in there?" When Shlomo shook his head, "No," Elie's fear turned to anger. What right had the police to take his watch, the present he had so recently received at his Bar Mitzvah? It meant much to him; why should he have to give it up so soon?

In the midst of the house searches and everyone's excitement, Moshe the Beadle ran into their house. Disheveled and breathless from running, he sought out Elie's father. "I warned you," he blurted out to Shlomo before he ran away again. This time, he did not come back.

After the three days of house arrest, everyone could leave their homes again. From now on, all Jews were forced to wear a large yellow star sewn on their clothing. No one would have any doubt about identifying a Jew. Elie was proud of being Jewish; the earlocks he wore to proclaim himself a pious Jewish boy meant a great deal to him. But it was different with this enforced Star of David. Elie cringed for the embarrassment it might cause the people he knew. He sensed their humiliation. Some of the most important people in the community—officials of the council, the rabbis, well-known merchants—all were suddenly dejected, deflated: targets.

Now every day brought another edict. Elie's family did not have to read the big announcements plastered on the circular street kiosks where people gathered to learn the news as soon as it was printed. Reb Shlomo, as a member of the community council, heard it even earlier.

Now Jews could no longer visit cafes or eat in restaurants. They could not travel on trains. They were forbidden to attend their synagogues for worship; they were not allowed on the streets after six in the evening.

The days followed each other. No one knew what to

expect next. Only for schoolboys was there a regular routine which made life appear somewhat normal. Jewish studies continued no matter what else happened.

Then came the next directive: all Jews in Sighet had to live in a section of the town separated from the rest of the population. In a ghetto. Barbed-wire fences would cut them off from contact with the Christian parts of town. Elie heard someone say it was just like the Middle Ages all over again.

Because there was another section where Jews lived, an outlying part of Sighet, two ghettos were set up: one for the people in the center of town, the other for the suburbs. People who lived elsewhere had to move into one of these ghettos.

Elie's family was fortunate. They could stay where they were. Their corner house was in the center of the town's Jewish district, and large enough to accommodate several displaced relatives who had to move in with them. Since their house fronted on a street located outside the ghetto, all windows on that side had to be boarded up.

People were beginning to believe that the ghetto was not too bad a change. At least here everyone was on the same level. Since they were all together and could not leave the area, they did not feel so vulnerable wearing the yellow star. If the Germans did not have any more evil tricks up their sleeves, they felt, it might be possible to sit out the war in this manner.

> Little by little life returned to normal. The barbed wire which fenced us in did not cause us any real fear. We even thought ourselves rather well off: we were entirely self-contained. A little Jewish republic.
>
> *(Night)*

Spring was unusually warm and pleasant. It was easy to believe that the harshest part of the German occupation might be over. After all, with the skies so blue and the breezes so gentle, how could men be unkind to each other?

It was a mild, calm Saturday evening, a week before Shavuot, an important Jewish festival occurring fifty days after the start of Passover. A large group of visitors had come to spend a few hours in the Wiesels' garden. They had come for the sake of companionship and diversion, for Shlomo Wiesel had a talent for telling good stories. He knew what was going on in the community, and his friends wanted to hear his thoughts on the current situation.

Even Elie was part of the socializing. Some of his friends had come with their parents; they sat in a small group by themselves, chatting.

In the midst of talking with his company, Shlomo received word that he must come to a meeting immediately. An urgent matter had arisen and he was wanted at an emergency gathering of the Jewish community council.

"Wait for me," Elie's father told his guests. "When I return, I shall tell you all about the meeting."

Most of the visitors stayed in the garden that night. They grew tense and worried as a long time elapsed without their host's returning. In the meantime rumors circulated throughout the ghetto. Other neighbors arrived, alarmed that something new was about to happen, frightened that it might be bad. As hours passed without Shlomo's return, conversation lagged; no one wanted to speculate on the cause for a meeting at such an unusual time. Finally only an occasional murmur broke the strained silence. Surrounded by the swaying of newly-budded tree branches, the Wiesels' visitors sat on their garden chairs, suddenly afraid of loud voices in the dark.

After midnight the garden gate opened and Elie's father came home. His face appeared paper-white in the darkness. As in a trance, Elie saw all the guests surround his father, wanting to know what had happened.

"I have terrible news," Shlomo Wiesel said, his voice a whisper, shocked by disbelief. "Deportation."

7

THAT NIGHT no one slept. The departure was to begin the following morning and there were some in the ghetto who had not yet heard the news.

Elie was one of the messengers sent around to knock on doors to notify the unaware that within a few hours they must be prepared to leave. Pack a few clothes, take some food, everyone was allowed to bring only one bag. A dazed look of disbelief met Elie on his rounds. Only when they saw the activity going on all about Sighet did some people realize the truth and slowly start getting their things together.

Meanwhile, one rumor chased after another: the presence of Jews so close to the war front presented a security problem to the Germans; all Jews from Transylvania were to be transported to other parts of Hungary, where they would work in factories. But no one really knew where they were to be sent, except for the head of the community council, and he was under threat of death not to reveal their destination.

Within a short time the ghetto was transformed into a beehive of frantic movement. In every house women cooked and baked, trying to produce as much food for their family's journey as their ovens could deliver. Every backyard became the depository for treasures that could not be taken along. Piles of books, carpets, linens cluttered the ground, already discarded and found to be unnecessary to their owners' survival.

In the Wiesel garden Elie looked on as his parents hastily dug hiding places at different locations: Reb Shlomo was leaving behind important papers and the jewelry he had not turned over to the police search parties, Elie's mother was burying her silver Shabbat candlesticks in the ground. Elie found a good place to keep his gold watch safe until the day they would all return and claim their belongings. He dug a deep hole under a tree near the fence and memorized the exact spot against the time when he would come back for the watch.

In the midst of so much haste and frenzy only the children were idle and silent. They did not know what to do with themselves while their parents and relatives were preparing for the next day, so they kept to themselves. Alone and forlorn, they did not wish to distress their elders any further.

It was during these last hours before dawn that someone knocked on the boarded-up window facing the street outside the ghetto. One of the newly-moved-in relatives of the Wiesels heard the knock and came running to tell them about it. Several people in the family worked rapidly to free the window so they could see who was there. But they were too late. The street outside the window was deserted, empty. Many years later Elie found out that a friend of his father's, an official with the Hungarian police, had come to warn them that night, hoping to help them escape. The warning might have saved them, had they heard it in time . . .

By ten o'clock the next morning the whole Jewish population stood lined up in the streets. Each house was emptied systematically by policemen who entered, ready to strike and beat with their clubs anyone who did not move fast enough. Since dawn the Jews had stood waiting, surrounded by their baggage, amid children crying of thirst in the heat of the summer's morning, while the police took roll call—once, twice, ten times. The people waited . . . and waited. Every single person in the ghetto had to be accounted for. For hours the police checked off names against their lists.

People were weary, from the lack of sleep the previous night, from sorting and packing, from the shock of the events befalling them. Even before they left their street older people and children were exhausted, sank down on their suitcases and bags.

The Wiesels were in the last group to move out. Shlomo had found out that from their house they would move into the smaller ghetto for a few days before their final departure.

When the signal finally came for the people in the street to move, Elie felt the whole scene to be unreal. As he and his parents stood behind their garden fence they watched a ghostly procession. Moving past were Elie's neighbors, his teachers, his rabbi, all the people who had held authority over him, whose teachings he had listened to and followed, those whom he had admired, feared, loved.

> They went by, fallen, dragging their packs, dragging their lives, deserting their homes, the years of their childhood, cringing like beaten dogs.
>
> *(Night)*

I saw them, unshaved, emaciated, bent; I saw them make their way, one sunny Sunday, toward the railroad station, destination unknown. I saw

"Zeide the Melamed," his too-heavy bundle bruising his shoulders. I was astonished: to think that this poor wanderer had once terrorized us.

And the "Selishter Rebbe," I saw him too in the middle of the herd, absorbed in his own private world as if in a hurry to arrive more quickly. . . . He was not weeping, his eyes no longer shot forth fire . . .

(*Legends of Our Time*, "My Teachers")

It did not seem possible, but it was there right before his eyes, the slow procession now leaving the ghetto; hundreds of people of all ages—from great-grandmothers to infants. Elie's whole world, the world of his fathers, moved past him. All he knew and remembered crept by as if in a trance.

It would soon be time for Shavuot, the festival of the giving of the Torah on Mount Sinai, but the Jews of Sighet would not be home to celebrate the holiday.

Seeing everyone moving past him had not really happened. It was Monday night and Elie was still in his house. He was falling asleep in the bed where he had slept every night of his life, within walls which knew his thoughts and had heard his prayers at the start of each day and when he closed his eyes in rest.

This was to be Elie's last night in his bed. He did not know where he would spend the nights after this. Tomorrow he would walk out of this house with his family for the last time, perhaps forever, and yet it did not seem possible. Even after seeing the others leave.

Elie wanted to push unhappy thoughts from his mind. He did not want to leave his home where he had felt safe. His body had grown here, his mind had stretched.

Whatever he was as a person was contained within these
rooms. This was his world, and that of his family. Outside
of it he was unknown, he did not matter.

He thought he would not sleep, but when he arose
early the following dawn he found he had slept after all.
He prayed earlier than usual, for it seemed especially
important to have enough time for the whole ritual this
day.

When, at nine o'clock, he heard the Hungarian police
shout on the street: "All Jews outside," his mind was more
at peace. He was ready.

Elie was the first of the family to walk out of the house.
It was easier to be first. He did not have to turn around to
look at the faces of his family. Looking at them would
make him cry, and this was no time for tears. Certainly
not in front of the police, who stood ready with their
clubs, waiting to hit anyone they could.

The street scene was familiar. It was identical to the one
they had witnessed two days before. The crowd bobbed
up and down. Standing up to be counted, checked against
the lists held by the police, sitting on the pavement
between the endless roll calls. Up, down, up, down. A
morning of waiting. A scene in slow motion.

And then it came—the order to march. It was almost a
relief after the long hours of waiting. It was also a
confirmation that the nightmare was reality. Once again
Elie saw people pick up their suitcases and their bundles.
Only this time it was his family. As he bent down to reach
for his belongings, Elie saw that his father was crying.

This was the first time in his life that Elie had seen his
father weep. It shocked him more than the exodus from
Sighet did. His father was the backbone of the family. He
had been the adviser of many people in the community.
He was strong, firm; others turned to him in their
troubles. But the forces of evil had taken over and Reb

Shlomo's parental authority was crumbling before Elie's eyes.

They moved into the other Jewish section of the city, into the smaller ghetto just vacated. There they stayed in the empty house of Elie's uncle for a few days. It was obvious that his uncle's family had been forced to leave without much warning: the kitchen was in disorder, traces of the last meal eaten by the family were left on the dishes still standing on the table.

Friday night was to be their last night before moving on themselves. It was eerie to light the Sabbath candles in a house not their own. It was upsetting to think about the former owners. Perhaps this would be the very last Sabbath they were spending together as a family. They really did not know where they were going, how they would live. For the Wiesels the ceremonies of that night, the blessing over the bread, the customary prayers, even the beautiful, familiar melodies they forced themselves to sing, went on as if in a trance, covering the private thoughts each person kept to himself.

Once again they were in the street the next morning. Only this time they knew for certain it was their last day here. Instead of the police, members of the Jewish community council handled the departure themselves. In silence everyone walked toward the large synagogue in Sighet, the gathering spot before leaving town.

It was a strange, silent human snake that wound its way around the town's market square. It was composed of hundreds of people, old and young, wise and simple, well-to-do and poverty-stricken, more alike than they had ever been while they lived together in Sighet. Now that they were leaving, their differences melted away.

There was strangeness in the silence of the town itself. It was as if no one else lived in Sighet. All the windows were shut tightly, as if their Christian neighbors wanted to blot out the sight of the departing Jews.

Not only were they being driven out of their homes; it seemed that no one cared. Not one face showed behind the shutters to bid a neighbor farewell. Not one voice was raised in protest. It was a scene from a dream: it was a bright, hot summer morning, and they were the last people on earth. Such an overwhelming feeling of being forsaken transmitted itself to the human snake that nothing was left to be said. Now there was only silence.

And yet, as he trudged alongside his parents, his sisters, and the little girl, Tzipora, Elie sensed that behind the closed shutters the inhabitants of the town were watching . . . and waiting.

All the houses left behind by the Jews of Sighet had open doors, inviting the general populace to come and help itself to the treasures left behind by that human snake now silently gliding out of town. The worldly goods which had been the property of the Jews of Sighet were still sitting in their houses, on their shelves, in their cellars—ready to be picked up by any stranger who walked through the gates of the now-empty ghetto. The precious trousseau silver of a housewife, a scholar's treasure of century-old books, recent gifts to a Bar Mitzvah boy—all these were exposed to the waiting hands of those invisible persons behind their curtains for whom the exodus in the street was perhaps not moving fast enough.

Whether by instinct or through teaching, the child Elie had felt well and accepted only amid his own people, among the things he knew. The uneasiness he had felt when walking near a church, the need to cross the street when the sidewalk was trod by the local priest, the cursing drunkenness of peasant bullies, the brute strength of the Hungarian police: these he had sensed and feared. But he had accepted them as a condition of the outside world.

If on a Friday night the very spirit of heaven seemed to descend upon the Jewish community of Sighet, there were other days when the very opposite was true. As a boy, Elie learned soon enough that two separate worlds lived within his town. The time for a Jew to find this out was on a major Christian holiday like Christmas or Easter. Then a Jew knew to stay inside his house, with the shutters closed tightly, for when the Hungarian peasant celebrated these religious holidays, he became even more intolerant than usual. The body-heating effect of a little holiday wine all too often led to the body-beating of a Jew who was caught out on the street.

Early in life, Elie was taught that the Jewish people were unique. The tragic events of their long history—the persecutions, the hatreds, the killings—were as much a part of their story as the ethics, the prophecies, the divine laws they had given to the world. Even while very young, Elie understood that people who think themselves different are disliked by others who do not share those differences. And so he had accepted the hostility—and his fear of it—as a normal occurrence of life in Sighet.

Of all the evils that assailed them on the day of their departure, Elie was most troubled by the apathy of the Christian population. For the rest of his life he was deeply troubled when remembering how the people of Sighet had stood by and, without a single murmur of dissent, allowed the expulsion of one-fourth of their population. How could anyone just *watch*? Watching, not doing anything, in the face of an injustice, he felt, was as much of a sin as actively engaging in a deed of evil.

Many years later Elie was to write about a person who

just watched, a silent witness. He called the story "Face in the Window" and incorporated it into his novel, *The Town Beyond the Wall*.

> My parents and I stood close to the fence: on the other side were life and liberty, or what men call life and liberty. . . . It was then that I saw him. A face in the window across the way. The curtains hid the rest of him; only his head was visible. It was like a balloon. Bald, flat nose, wide empty eyes. A bland face, banal, bored; no passion ruffled it. I watched it for a long time. It was gazing out, reflecting no pity, no pleasure, no shock, not even anger or interest. Impassive, cold, impersonal. The face was indifferent to the spectacle. . . .
>
> His face, empty of all expression, followed me for long years. I have forgotten many others, not his. . . .
>
> The spectator is entirely beyond us. He sees without being seen. He is there but unnoticed. The footlights hide him. He never applauds nor hisses; his presence is evasive, and commits him less than his absence might. He says neither yes nor no, and not even maybe. He says nothing. He is there, but he acts as if he were not. Worse: he acts as if the rest of us were not.

Most Saturday mornings of his life Elie had gone to Sighet's main synagogue with his father. He had not felt as warm at these services, often looking forward to the evening, when he would attend the third Sabbath meal at the shtibel of the Hasidic rebbe across the street. But he had been a dutiful son, standing beside Shlomo while they prayed in the large, liberal sanctuary that his father preferred to attend.

Elie stood beside his father again in the main synagogue, only this time he did not pray. It was the destiny of
Sighet's Jews that their last station in town was to be the
main synagogue.

The irony of spending their last day, which happened to
be a Saturday, in the synagogue was not lost on anyone.
Also the use to which the sanctuary was put on that day.

Shlomo and Elie were downstairs with the rest of the
men; Elie's mother and sisters were in the women's
gallery upstairs. They were separated as if for a religious
service. There the ghastly semblance ended.

The synagogue was no longer a house of worship. So
many people were crowded into it that it resembled a
huge barn. The pews could not accommodate such an
overwhelming assembly, so most people took turns standing up.

Where the bima had once stood, suitcases and bundles
now littered the hall. The wall hangings and the Torah
curtains which had sheltered the holy ark had all been
removed. With them sanctity and dignity had gone out.

Hungarian police stood guard outside. No one was
allowed to leave the building, even to use the outdoor
toilets. People had no alternative but to relieve themselves in the corners of the synagogue. In the heat of the
summer day the stench and the lack of fresh air soon made
it hard to breathe.

The German plan was thorough. It had anticipated
every step, from the establishment of ghettos in which all
the Jews were kept together to the use of lists by which
each person could be accounted for: in all of Eastern
Europe, in towns large and small, Jewish communities
were being rounded up in identical fashion. The people of
one did not know what was happening in any other: also
part of the plan.

In the synagogue Elie stayed close to his father, who

was moving around in the crowd, reassuring and comforting others. Once in a while it was possible to exchange signals with the rest of the family in the gallery upstairs, but only a slight wave of arms was seen from one to the other. There was no voice communication. Too many people occupied every inch of space, nibbling on their food supplies, praying, dozing, whispering to each other.

The inactivity and the uncertainty of what lay ahead made the next twenty-four hours of waiting in the synagogue agony for all. Surely, nothing facing them in the future could be as bad as this.

The Main Synagogue of Sighet As Elie Knew It As a Child

Permission to reproduce stills from the film Sighet, Sighet *courtesy of The Images Film Archive*

Jews' Street in Sighet, Closed Up and Deserted after Its Occupants Were Forced to Leave. It Was Renamed Street of the Deported.

8

THE NEXT MORNING the last group of Jews, which included the Wiesel family, was marched to the railroad station. The dazed crowd was pushed toward a long row of freight cars waiting on the siding. Elie and his father were together with his mother and his sisters again, and Elie edged close to them. The Hungarian police were counting off eighty people to each car and he was petrified that he might become separated from his family.

It took no time to fill the cars. The doors were sealed, a whistle blew, and the train moved out of the station. No one knew where it was headed. Through a tiny crack in the side of their car, Elie saw several black-uniformed SS men. They were smiling. One of the officers striding up and down the station platform was a Colonel Adolf Eichmann, who had come to Sighet to supervise the execution of a plan known as the "final solution."

The journey was Elie's first venture out of town, except for the yearly vacation trips his family had taken to nearby mountain resorts and his annual visit to Debreczin for his high school exams. This trip, however, was nothing like those summer excursions with their expectations of hikes in the country, picking strawberries in the woods, or stopping at outdoor restaurants for ice cream. This time, Elie's baggage was composed of a few items of clothing and his set of phylacteries, and his expectations were based on fear.

Elie thought of Martha, their old family servant, forced to leave them when the ghetto was set up and Christians were no longer allowed to work for Jewish employers. Just a few days before, Martha had slipped into the ghetto for a visit with them. She had offered the Wiesels refuge in her home village, but Shlomo had turned down her offer. As a community leader, he felt, he should stay in Sighet with his wife and their little girl, but if Elie and the older girls wanted to go with her . . . Of course, they had decided to stay with their parents.

Gradually the people on the train used up the food they had brought along. There had been a few buckets of water when they entered the car, but it did not last long. The lack of space in the car, and the summer heat, made them very thirsty.

After a few hours, the train halted at a little station, which they recognized as a town near the Czechoslovakian border. They were traveling in the opposite direction from the one they had expected! Suddenly everyone aboard understood that the illusion was over: they were not being moved away from the war front; they were not going to work in any Hungarian factories.

While the train stood in the station, the door slid open. A German army officer strode into their car. From now on, he snapped at them, they were under the authority of the German army. At that moment their worst fears emerged into the open. Their destination was not to be a peaceful spot where they would await the outcome of the war. Simultaneously the people on the train plunged into icy despair: they were being transported out of the country. That could only mean the worst.

From all corners of Europe freight cars filled with Jews were rolling eastward toward Poland, each sealed train headed for a no-return destination. The people impris-

oned on those trains did not know of each other, nor
would it have helped them.

For four days and nights the train carrying Elie's family
rolled across the Polish countryside. Inside, each person
fought his own shock and helplessness. Then the train
stopped.

> . . . we had reached a station. Those who were next
> to the windows told us its name:
> "Auschwitz."
> No one had ever heard that name.

> *(Night)*

The train sat on the tracks all that day. Later that same
night, it moved again. When it finally stopped, the people
in the freight cars saw bright flames outside, flames which
shot out from a high chimney stack. Immediately, they
smelled a horrible odor which had crept into the car. It
smelled of burning flesh.

At midnight the doors of the freight car were flung
open. In the semi-darkness, gangs of men, dressed in
striped tunics and dark trousers, swooped in, shining
their big flashlights at the frightened occupants, yelling at
them to get out fast. They swung their clubs at everyone
within reach, hitting those who did not move quickly. The
Wiesels, too, spilled out of the train, dragging themselves
onto a huge station platform, where every few feet SS
men with drawn guns and snarling dogs on leashes
covered the crowd. They had arrived at Birkenau, reception center for the larger camp of Auschwitz.

The huge mass of people emerging from the long train
was pushed forward until the length of the platform was
covered. Suddenly, a single SS officer, holding a club,
stepped in front of them:

"Men to the left! Women to the right!"

Silently two separate lines were formed. Holding on to his father's arm in desperation, Elie saw his mother and his sisters walk to the right, away from them. The line to the right moved rapidly. As Elie saw his mother disappear from his view, he noticed that she was holding young Tzipora with one hand, stroking her hair with the other as if to quiet the small girl's fears. For the rest of his life Elie was to remember that midnight moment when his mother was lost to him. He was never able to accept that a few words uttered so casually and so totally without emotion by a German noncommissioned officer could separate them forever.

Elie's agony and sense of utter helplessness were beyond words. After that, basic animal fear took over, fear that he would be separated from his father too, severing the last family link. Whatever else might happen, Elie was determined to stay with his father.

The line of men and boys was soon pushed off the platform and found itself on an endless, wide road throbbing with a sea of people who had arrived on trains before them. To their right, now, were the trains. On the left of the road a deep ditch paralleled the walkway. A high electrified fence ran beside the ditch as far as the eye could see.

They walked five abreast, their steps lighted eerily in the darkness by flames shooting out of the tall chimney stacks looming ahead of them on the right. The bizarre events of the night were compounded by the warnings of veteran prisoners who stood in the shadows by the side of the road and tried to prepare the newcomers in the best way they knew: brutal and harsh. In rough voices they told the new people that they would be burned alive in the furnaces straight ahead of them. One prisoner even jumped in front of Elie and asked his age. Elie was fifteen and said so. "No, no, eighteen," the man yelled hoarsely at Elie. "Eighteen, you fool." In the same manner Shlomo was told to reduce his age from fifty to forty, before his adviser was swallowed in darkness again.

In the line behind Shlomo and Elie, loud murmurs of protest broke out. Some of the younger men in the crowd carried knives on their persons. Their voices erupted in anger: "Why should we allow ourselves to be led to the slaughter like this? Better to go down fighting than to let them take us to their furnaces." The sentiment Elie heard most clearly was: "Wait till the world hears what is really going on in Auschwitz."

But there were older voices, calming voices, in the crowd. They told their children that it was not the teaching of their religion to rebel against their fate.

"Do not lose faith," Elie heard, "even when the sword hangs over your head."

Soon the crowd surged onto a large open space. Standing in the middle of a square, holding a conductor's baton, was an SS officer with a monocle clamped into one eye. Surrounded by other SS officers, Dr. Josef Mengele was holding court. By pointing his baton to left or right, he determined the fate of every prisoner who stepped in front of him. At the moment when he approached Dr. Mengele, Elie had no idea which direction meant death and which meant life. He remembered to say eighteen when Dr. Mengele asked his age. He replied yes when asked if he were in good health. Occupation? "Farmer." He had almost said "student." The baton pointed to the left.

Elie waited anxiously to see where his father would be sent. No matter where the baton pointed for Shlomo, Elie intended to go that way too. He was relieved when his father was directed to the left. Even if it meant going to the crematoria, at least they would be together.

Now the march continued, headed toward a huge flame arising from a ditch in front of them. Perhaps the prisoners who had warned them that they were going to the crematoria were right.

As Elie's eyes focused on the fire, he saw a sight he would never forget. A large truck pulled up and discharged a load—a human load—right into the fiery pit. Babies, little children . . . was he seeing right? Surely this was a nightmare and he would awake, back home in his bed, among his books, and find that none of this had happened.

Elie had been trained to believe in God. He had been taught that God played an active role in the life of men, and all his thinking had been directed toward faith in God's special relationship with the Jewish people. Despite all this, Elie suddenly found that he was no more prepared than anyone else for what he was experiencing at Auschwitz. All through his first night there he asked himself over and over: How could anyone burn little children? How could the world permit such deeds? How could a God exist and not stop such evil? Everyone who stumbled through the dark of the Auschwitz night, illuminated by the lights of hell blazing from the chimneys, asked himself the same questions. Not a single soul found an answer—there could be none. There had never been a scene like this in all of human history.

The crowd of men and boys—Elie and his father among them—trudged forward. At the end of the road they saw a larger burning pit. This one, Elie knew, would consume them. He looked to his father for comfort, hoping that, as always, Shlomo would have reassurance of some kind for him. Suddenly, Elie needed to be a child again, he needed a father who could take his troubles away. But his father looked dazed. He muttered that it was a shame Elie had not gone with his mother; he had seen other boys of Elie's age go with their mothers.

As they straggled on, Elie tried to reverse roles and reassure his father. Humanity would not permit such a situation to occur, he told him. But Shlomo Wiesel had given up. In the face of this horror, he had lost his belief in man.

In a choked voice, Shlomo told Elie that anything was possible. Humanity did not care about them. Even these crematoria were possible. At this response, Elie became completely desperate. He looked about and decided that he would end his life by running onto the electrified barbed-wire fence. Better that than to face the slow agony of the flames. He started telling his father of his decision, but he was not sure Shlomo even heard him. His father's lips were moving, his body was shaking with sobs. The lips of every man and boy near them moved, and Elie recognized that they were all saying the Kaddish, the Hebrew prayer for the dead. He saw the moving lips, the bodies bending in reverence, and wondered whether there had ever been another time in the long history of his people when this prayer, meant to be said over the dead, had to be uttered by the dying for themselves. No one would come after them. No one would mourn them or pray for their souls. Or glorify the name of God.

Where was God? Had they left Him outside the gates? Did He care about what was happening to His people?

Step by step they approached the large burning ditch. Elie said a silent goodbye to all he knew. He said goodbye to his father too, in his heart, for he could not address Shlomo openly to tell him. Elie's father was weeping. Elie could not weep. In his mind he planned how he would dash to the fatal fence at the exact second they approached the ditch. As if by automatic reflex, his lips, too, whis-

pered the words of the Kaddish: "Yisgadal Veyiskadash—
May His name be blessed and magnified."

Two steps before they arrived at the ditch, the guards
ordered everyone to turn left. Looming up in the darkness ahead of them stood several barracks. These were
their destination.

9

LIKE A SLEEPWALKER, Elie stumbled into the barracks, not certain whether the events of this night were real or imagined. He had just been given a last-minute reprieve from the burning ditches. Now he stood inside a huge enclosure which resembled a horse stall. The whole building was lined with a triple-layer of wooden slats: sleeping accommodations for one thousand men. Elie was so dreadfully tired that he longed to walk over to one of these platforms and curl up and close his eyes. But he was not allowed to sleep.

In groups of three hundred, the men were greeted by veteran prisoners, armed with rubber truncheons, who ordered them to get out of their clothes. Blows rained down on those who did not comply rapidly enough. Leaving their garments behind, the new men were then driven to another end of the barracks where they ran through hot showers and were doused with heavy doses of disinfectants. They then stood naked in the night air, shivering. It was hours before they were ordered to run to yet another barracks, where their prison clothing was issued to them. At no point during the long night did anyone receive any food, nor were they allowed to rest, or even to sit on the ground. At one point, Elie later remembered, he actually dozed off while on his feet, his eyes wide open.

Staring at the long line of bluish-colored skylights

running the length of the barracks, Elie concentrated on the one thought which nagged at him constantly: he must not become separated from his father. As he fixed his eyes on the windows overhead, it seemed to him that their light was becoming brighter. Was this long night actually coming to an end?

During the many hours of "processing," SS officers circulated among the prisoners, looking them over in their nudity as if they were prize specimens in a cattle market. The SS officers were looking for strong men. It was another "selection," another test like the one they had undergone when Dr. Mengele had waved them toward one side, the side which meant they would live.

Was it better to pretend to be strong, or was it better to remain anonymous and not draw attention to oneself?

Somehow, Shlomo communicated to Elie that he thought it better if they remained unnoticed. Together, he and Elie stood still, as inconspicuous as possible, while the SS officers picked out a number of healthy-looking men from their group.

Not much later Elie was to thank his father for having made the right choice during this first test in a system meant to destroy them. The "strong men" selected from their midst became part of the Sonderkommando, a special work force with duties in the crematories. Most of them would not live long.

The technique of remaining anonymous became Elie's lifeline. It was especially important when dealing with the kapos—veteran prisoners who were in charge of the newcomers and policed them. For the majority of the inmates the kapos were the only level of camp administration with which they came into direct contact.

Most of the kapos were political prisoners, some were former criminals. Some came from German-occupied countries, some were even Jewish. All the kapos owed their lives and well-being to the fact that they ruled the other prisoners for the SS, the Schutzstaffel, the black-uniformed security troops who ran the camps. The degree of efficiency with which they did their job earned the kapos small favors from the SS, such as larger food rations, but especially important, an overwhelming power over the life and death of the inmates in their charge.

Elie soon found out that the kapos were more brutal than the Germans in their dealings with fellow prisoners. Because they knew they were hated, having sold themselves to the enemy, the kapos took out their aggressive feelings on their victims whenever they could, and they used every chance to get even. Elie and Shlomo discovered quickly that it was best to remain as invisible as possible in the sight of a kapo. Being conspicuous only led to trouble.

After standing in the night air for hours, Shlomo developed strong stomach cramps. In desperation, he stepped out of line and walked up to the guard, an ill-tempered gypsy, in charge of the prisoners. Politely, Shlomo addressed the guard in German:

"Would you please show me the way to the toilets?"

The gypsy did not answer. He looked Shlomo up and down several times. Then, still without uttering a word, he hit Shlomo in the face with his fist. Shlomo fell to the ground. He lay there without moving for several moments.

Elie stared down in horror, too shocked to move. Soon, he felt the blood rush to his head, and his body turned hot with shame. How could he witness his father's degradation and not act? Was it not his duty to avenge Shlomo by knocking down the aggressor? But all Elie could do was to stare, as his father slowly rose to his feet, rubbing a large red mark on his cheek with one hand. Just one day at camp and he had changed. Had the dehumanizing atmosphere of this place begun to work on him already? Elie felt terrible. The feeling did not go away even after Shlomo assured him that it really did not hurt much.

A half-hour's distance from the reception camp of Birkenau lay the main camp of Auschwitz. Five abreast, Elie's whole group was marched to Auschwitz early one dawn, without previous warning. Gypsies guarded the prisoners with special care. They cracked whips around the ankles of the marchers, and with their truncheons eagerly clubbed any stragglers who fell behind.

A huge banner over the entrance to Auschwitz greeted the marchers when they reached the barbed-wire electrified fence: "Work is Liberty." Once inside, the prisoners once again were surrounded by SS men with machine guns and snarling dogs on leashes.

Already, Elie knew the truth of those words over the gate. No one walked out of this gate alive. Those who made it this far worked. Once a prisoner grew weak and ill, there was only one escape route: through the chimneys. Even from here, they could see the brownish-black clouds hovering over the camp, spewed out by the smokestacks of the crematoria. The greasy black ash raining down on the marchers was proof. The slow thick rain tasted and smelled of bitter almonds.

Instead of wooden barracks, the compound of Auschwitz consisted of acres and acres of two-story concrete buildings, separated from each other by high fences of electrified barbed wire. The main camp of Auschwitz furnished the manpower for the many slave-labor camps surrounding it. Elie prayed for strength for Shlomo and himself.

Once again, the prisoners underwent the routine of hot

showers and disinfection, then sat naked in the cold night air for hours while awaiting assignment to a permanent block. Elie was to find out that this procedure took place every time prisoners were moved from one place to another.

At Block 17, to which he was assigned in Auschwitz, Elie and his group were received by a young Polish prisoner, who told his charges not to despair, but to have faith. Hell is not forever, he told them, and faith will drive away death. Above all, he advised the new prisoners, be comrades to one another. All of them were suffering the same fate; helping each other would help keep them alive. It was the most humane speech Elie had yet heard in the camp. That night, he slept a little more peacefully.

The next day, Elie lined up outside his block for roll call. The men in the long columns were told to roll up their sleeves. They moved slowly toward a small wooden table. When Elie's turn came, he stood before three prisoners manning tatoo needles. One of them engraved a number on the inside of his left forearm. Elie Wiesel became prisoner #A-7713.

From then on, his identity was left behind; he was known by a number. Whenever he had occasion to speak to a guard or any other camp authority, whether to make a request or reply to a question, he had to address that person by his full title and announce himself as "Prisoner Number A-7713."

For three weeks the new inmates did not have to work. It was good to have a little extra sleep, even a nap outside their block in the afternoon. But as, one by one, the long barracks were emptied of their occupants and only Elie's group remained in camp, he and his fellow inmates became worried. If they had no skills, they were useless to their captors; that meant their days were numbered.

They almost envied the people who had already been shipped out to other camps: at least they had an immediate future.

Then the kind Pole, their block head, was replaced. Apparently he had not been sufficiently brutal to his charges. His replacement made up in savagery what the Pole had lacked. The assistants to the new block leader imitated their chief's ruthlessness. Together, they saw to it that every action in their barracks made nonpersons out of the individuals in their charge. All rules had to be obeyed instantly and unquestioningly. Soon the prisoners became childlike creatures, without wills of their own.

The teen-aged prisoner #A-7713, dressed in black-and-white striped prison garb, owned a bar of soap, a soup bowl, and the knife and spoon issued to him by the camp authorities. Twice a day, at dawn and at dusk, he lined up in the long ranks outside his block and stood for roll call. There were about one thousand prisoners in each block. They stood until the SS had checked the number of every single man on the list.

The day began at dawn. Breakfast was a tin cup filled with the vile, dark liquid which passed as coffee. At noon, the main meal consisted of a bowl of soup. The prisoners received a ration of bread after the evening roll call. At nine o'clock, it was bedtime.

In the dehumanizing process which was the aim of the concentration camp, Elie learned an important lesson from his father. Once, after they had been given their evening's ration of bread, Shlomo said to him, "Don't eat it all at once. Remember, tomorrow's another day."

Elie was too starved to mind his father's advice that day. But he came to understand that Shlomo wanted him to know that one could retain some small control over one's life, even in camp. By deciding just when he would swallow the allotted ration, a prisoner could still assert himself as an individual.

Some of the others, meanwhile, had their own methods of remaining human. Among the inmates who had come from Sighet, one man had been able to smuggle a pair of tefillin into Auschwitz. Every dawn, before the majority of prisoners arose for morning roll call, he and several others among the pious in the group were up and standing in a row facing a barracks wall. While the owner of the phylacteries adjusted them on his arm, all recited the blessing: "Blessed are You, Lord our God, King of the Universe, Who has sanctified us with His commandments and commanded us to wear tefillin."

When the worshipper arranged the section of the phylacteries worn on the head, all blessed that step of the ritual by reciting together: "Blessed be the Name of His glorious majesty for ever and ever."

Then they were ready for morning prayers. Elie, although he participated in the laying of tefillin, had stopped praying. He could no longer feel the personal connection between God and himself which had been so special to him before. Since the night he had left the transport train in Birkenau, Elie had been questioning the justice of a God who allowed the depravity and torture he had witnessed. Elie did not deny the existence of God, but he could no longer praise Him. During those first few weeks of camp life, Elie was painfully aware that his childhood had been stolen from him, and with it, the faith he had valued so highly.

10

ELIE'S GROUP was moved from Auschwitz. A four-hour march brought the prisoners to the labor camp of Buna, where all the men in Elie's unit, consisting mostly of Hungarians, were assigned to jobs which they, as unskilled workers, could do.

Elie felt himself fortunate. He worked at an inside job in a factory warehouse where electrical parts were sorted. Shlomo worked near him in the same place. Elie was grateful that he could keep an eye on Shlomo and protect him as much as possible.

Sometimes in the evening, when roll call was over but it was still light outside, Shlomo and Elie played chess in their bunk. The chessmen were obtained at a high price: they were made of bread crumbs hoarded from the daily ration. The decision to play chess meant making do with even less than they had already. It was at such times that Shlomo mentioned Elie's mother and sisters. He wondered about them aloud, musing that since they were strong, and Elie's mother still a young woman, they were probably in a labor camp too. Shlomo's words hurt Elie. He thought of those first few days, of the chimneys in Birkenau, and felt it most unlikely that his mother and sisters had survived them. But he pretended for his father's sake, aware they were only playing games with each other. They were keeping up each other's hopes.

But most of the time the mind-numbing fatigue of their sixteen-hour workdays, and the little food they received, made it an effort to think of their loved ones. Days went by when all the thought Elie could muster was focused on the moment when he would be allowed to fall on his wooden plank in total exhaustion.

One particular occasion arose when Elie thought he could help his father. In his youth, Shlomo had never received any military training; he had never learned to march in cadence. But in the concentration camp the prisoners were always moved from place to place in military style. Each work group which left camp in the morning, every one returning to the barracks at night, marched in step. Shlomo was forever out of step. This gave the kapos an excuse for hitting him every time they noticed him.

One of the kapos held a particular grievance against Elie. He had discovered that Elie's front tooth was gold-capped, and he wanted that gold. The kapo also knew of Elie's concern for his father, so, naturally, he focused his vengeance on Shlomo, a helpless target. To save his father from the kapo's aggression, Elie decided to teach Shlomo how to march properly.

Every evening for two whole weeks, Shlomo and Elie practiced marching outside the barracks amid the derision of their fellow prisoners. Elie gave the commands, his father marched. But it didn't work. Shlomo was too tired, too defeated, to learn anything new. He could not keep the cadence, nor did he know how to change step when Elie ordered him to. Finally, even Elie had to admit it was no use. The kapo had won; now he wanted his prize. Elie knew better than to refuse him. Shlomo would be the victim of his stubbornness. On an evening shortly afterward, Elie underwent "dental surgery" in the latrine. A Jewish dentist from Warsaw performed the tooth extraction with a rusty spoon, and Elie handed the gold crown over to his father's tormentor.

Public beatings were so frequent in the camp that precise rules existed for them. The allowed maximum was twenty-five strokes with a leather whip administered to a victim spread out over a box, face down. Elie had witnessed enough such procedures to know that a beating always took place in the open, before the culprit's block-mates.

Early one evening, work was stopped sooner than usual and roll call was held on the spot instead of on the grassy plot in front of the barracks. When the kapo called out: "A-7713," Elie knew instinctively what was in store for him. Just a few days before, he had done the unpardona-ble. He had accidentally surprised a kapo in the act of making love. The furious kapo had caught him before he could run away and angrily threatened that he would be punished. Now that punishment was about to take place. The kapo made a short speech: "An ordinary prisoner has no right to meddle in other people's affairs. One of you does not seem to have understood this. I'm obliged, therefore, to make it very clear to him once and for all."

(Night)

Elie heard the guard count the strokes. He was aware of twenty-three blows to his body; during the last two he lost consciousness. He was revived by a bucket of cold water thrown over him as he lay on the ground. Even then, his only thought was that his father must be suffering terribly to see him in such a situation.

When the job in the warehouse was completed, Elie became part of another labor unit. Now, most of his day was spent out of doors. He dug the soil, moved bricks, loaded freight trains. He thought himself fortunate.

Beside him worked a scholar, the former head of a yeshiva, and Elie became his pupil. At the height of the summer heat the old man, who had never done any hard physical labor before, and Elie, who had wanted to become a rabbi, kept their souls alive by reciting portions of Talmud to each other. Their effort to reconstruct whole pages from memory helped them to forget the present, the hunger, and the horror. Talmud was their life-preserver: amid the extreme terror, they found that their minds still functioned and that they had retained knowledge from a previous life. For Elie's teacher, having a student sustained his will to live. For Elie, it was a reason to keep going, nourished by the admonition which Dodye Feig had left with him: "You are Jewish, your task is to remain Jewish. The rest is up to God."

"When the war is over, we'll take the first ship to Haifa." That was Elie's dream. He shared it with two friends, Tibi and Yossi, a pair of brothers from Czechoslovakia, who slept in the same bunk with him. Before falling asleep in the darkness of the barracks, the brothers and Elie often spoke about going to Palestine. Sometimes, they sang Hebrew songs while sitting on the top of their bunk. They sang softly so no kapo would hear them and beat them into silence with his truncheon. The boys took pleasure in imagining the golden future which would be theirs in Palestine. Tibi and Yossi had attended secret Zionist youth meetings in their hometown and there learned many wondrous stories about Eretz Yisrael which they now shared with Elie. He was reminded of his friend Yerachmiel, who also had spoken of the Holy Land with such ardor.

Every night, before falling asleep on his wooden plank covered with a bit of straw, Elie fixed his thoughts on the Jordan Valley, on the green fields of the Galilee, on the glories of the city of Jerusalem. The hope that he would one day see these places kept him alive and comforted him.

When a particular day in camp had been intolerable, the presence of a devout Jew named Akiba Drumer gave the inmates of their block a spiritual uplift. He, like the rest of their group, came from Hungary and knew some of the Wishnitzer niggunim, the Hasidic chants of their region. His singing brought back thoughts of home to them all, but it also reminded them that their current trial was but one segment in the long history of their people. Akiba had some kabbalistic background; he was constantly searching for signs announcing the day of their liberation. For the discouraged, beaten men of Block 36, it was good to know that one person among them still had faith in God and hope for the future.

Few days were easy that summer. It was always a surprise to finish the day of laboring with the building unit, come back to the barracks for the soup and roll call, and find one's friends still around. When Elie was put into the labor squad, he had been separated from his father and moved into another barracks. Now his first move upon returning to camp every evening was to check on Shlomo. Deep inside, there was always the fear that something had happened to his father during his absence, that Shlomo had not made it through the day.

There were evenings when the return to camp had dire consequences. Several times that summer the camp inmates had to witness executions. Assembled in the open, surrounded by armed guards and fenced in by electrified barbed wire, the thousands of prisoners stood at attention, their heads uncovered, while they faced the gallows erected in the center of the yard. Each time there was an execution, it was obvious that it was an object lesson, a warning to every prisoner that the same fate could await him if he violated any camp rules. Nothing was spared the onlooker, not even the final march past the gallows for everyone, forced to observe at close range the corpse dangling at the end of the rope. Although death surrounded the inmates at every moment of the day, although everyone at Auschwitz knew that the crematories were working full blast night and day, to Elie the hangings still brought the worst share of horror. People disappeared, or were removed through the frequent "selections," or simply died from starvation and exhaustion. But the actual witnessing of a death left an undeniable impact.

One case in particular touched not only Elie, but everyone present, deep to the soul. It was the execution of a young boy, the servant of a kapo foreman. The kapo had been found guilty in connection with an act of espionage within the camp, and by association, blame was put upon the boy, a very handsome youth whom Elie recalled as the "sad angel" because of the expression in his eyes. This boy had been beloved by all who had come into contact with him; his ordeal touched many hearts in the camp. Of the many nightmarish experiences Elie had in concentration camps, the execution of the "sad angel" was an episode he never forgot.

> Behind me, I heard the same man asking:
>   "Where is God now?"
>   And I heard a voice within me answer him:
>   "Where is He? He is—He is hanging here on this gallows. . . ."
>   That night the soup tasted of corpses.
>
> *(Night)*

As the summer days passed and autumn approached, the prisoners talked of the coming of the Jewish New Year.

Elie dreaded the thought. He, to whom the High Holy Days had meant the high point of the year, was filled with the most negative thoughts. It was a complete reversal of everything he had felt only last year at this time. Then, he had believed that his fervent prayers were the direct key to God. It had been up to him—through the intensity with which he appealed to God—to influence Him, to ask Him for blessings for his family and for himself. Elie's belief had undergone the most drastic of changes. Not only had he been disappointed by God; after the cruel events which had befallen them during the past year, Elie had every reason to doubt the very existence of God. His whole former life had been a love affair with the idea of a beneficent God. His every day had been devoted to the service of religion. But now . . .

On the eve of Rosh Hashana at Buna, close to ten thousand Jews stood in the open assembly area where they congregated only for camp roll calls or for hangings. In the confines of the barbed-wire fences, under the observation of smirking SS men and armed soldiers, the voice of a rabbi led them, without the use of prayerbooks, in observing the start of a new year. The very idea was absurd. Who among them would be around for another twelve months? Every day was begrudged to them. How, then, could they ask God, the Father and King, for a year of life?

Had it only been a year since he stood with Dodye Feig at the service of the Bonsher Rebbe in Sighet, swaying with emotion and reverence, praying for the welfare of his family and of the world? He did not know where his grandfather was now; Dodye's deportation had taken place separately from theirs. His mother, his sisters, little Tzipora . . . he knew where they had gone. His own eyes had seen them walk out of his life.

Here everyone was reciting the Kaddish—for their

loved ones, for their friends, for their past. Even this prayer was an affirmation of God, for it praised and glorified Him, expressed faith in His justice, and in the meaningfulness of life.

Darkness fell over the assembly square. The vast crowd did not want to disperse. After attending this emotional service, held in the very jaws of hell, the men did not want to break away from each other. Only the bell for bedtime forced them back to their barracks.

Elie had not been able to pray. He had mouthed the familiar words, but he had not prayed. He could not pray to someone who had disappointed him so grievously, who had rewarded devotion so hideously, who had pulled his world from under him. God, he felt, owed him an apology for betraying all his years of faith and trust.

Elie felt himself all burned out. Everything he had believed was now lying dead inside him. On this sacred day, he felt only anger. Against God, against fate. It was a useless rebellion. It helped no one; it made no one feel good. In the darkness of the Rosh Hashana evening, Elie felt completely alone in the universe. He was alone and cold, and his soul was dead. In all the fifteen years of his life, he had never felt so awful.

It would have been unthinkable before to even consider not fasting on Yom Kippur, the Day of Atonement. The very idea would have been blasphemy to a religious Jew. Now that this Holy Day was upon them, here in camp where every effort was bent toward extinguishing both the religion and its practitioners, the choice weighed heavily on all the inmates.

With the loss of even one day's ration of soup and bread, a prisoner could easily become so weak that he would die. Whether this practical consideration should sway one in favor of eating, and thereby rebelling against God, was a difficult decision to make. Perhaps it was better to fast, knowing that a quick clean death would result.

In their discussions, Pinhas, the man whose pupil Elie had become, said he would eat, in defiance of a God who had brought them to such a fate. Elie was shaken to find that such a man of strong faith as Pinhas had also lost his belief. As for himself, Elie had been ordered by his father not to fast.

When Kol Nidre night arrived, all the men hurried to their barracks after returning from their work shifts and cleaned up in preparation for their service. A fear that the SS might do them harm—a favorite trick for use on Jewish holidays—kept the prisoners from conducting their sacred service outdoors as they had done for Rosh Hashana. This time each block congregated separately and was led in prayers by a cantor. The service was uniform throughout the camp: it had been prepared by a group of religious men who had transcribed prayers from memory onto jealously guarded sheets of toilet paper. Each barracks was, therefore, reciting the same prayers at the same time.

Elie went through the service mechanically. He recited the familiar prayers, but his mind questioned their contents. Why, he wondered, should anyone in this place need to atone for sins when they were themselves blameless victims of sin rather than sinners? He mouthed words which had come down through the ages and inwardly asked whether these prayers from another time could possibly apply to the situation in which he and all the other prisoners now found themselves.

He felt betrayed, and at the same time he was betraying. The following day, Yom Kippur Day, when he was back working at the digging detail, Elie ate the soup ration and nibbled the dry bread doled out to him. And felt nothing.

The selection which they had feared would happen during Yom Kippur came shortly afterwards. Once again the dreaded Dr. Mengele came to their block, watched a parade of naked men pass before him, and noted down the numbers of those whom he considered too weak, too ill, or too old to be of further use to the camp. Elie was petrified by the thought that his father's turn had come. Shlomo had aged incredibly during the summer. It was obvious to Elie that he was a beaten man. His heart beat fast at the thought that this would be just as obvious to the camp authorities, who needed no excuse to get rid of anyone unable to work.

Elie went through torment during the day on which those chosen at the last selection were to be shipped out. Shlomo's number had been noted down: he was on the dreaded list.

> I did not know myself what I wanted—for the day to pass quickly or not. I was afraid of finding myself alone that night. How good it would be to die here!
>
> At last we began the return journey. How I longed for orders to run!
>
> The military march. The gate. The camp.
>
> I ran to Block 36.
>
> Were there still miracles on this earth? He was alive. He had escaped the second selection. He had been able to prove that he was still useful.
>
> *(Night)*

Shlomo had been among the fortunate ones. Akiba Drumer was not. The prophet who had shared his belief in a happier future with all his blockmates had lost his strength. When his body wore out, so did his soul. He was among those condemned to die by Dr. Mengele.

Pinhas, Elie's work partner and teacher, was another who did not survive. The old rabbi had fasted, after all, on Yom Kippur Day. With a sad smile he had explained to Elie that his reason for doing so was not the same as his reason for fasting on previous Days of Atonement. This time it had been as an act of defiance.

The winds blew cold on the remaining inmates of the camp as the days of autumn drew to a close and cold weather arrived. To Elie it seemed as if those winds blew the last remaining bit of faith right out of the camp gates.

11

On the September day when he turned sixteen, Elie considered himself fortunate to still be alive, even more to have his father still among the living. Yet, with an early winter on its way, he wondered how either of them would survive the coming months. As the days grew shorter and the nights longer and colder, life became hopeless and close to unbearable. Early snows and icy winds whipped up the northern part of Europe. The prisoners were issued their winter uniforms: a heavier shirt than the one they had worn in summer. Their rations of bread and thin soup remained the same.

Elie had no long conversations with his father, but felt closer to him than at any previous time. In this desperate time, both tried hard to look out for one another; each gave the other an incentive for living, for holding on a little bit longer.

The hours at dawn when they had to stand outside for roll call were physically painful. After a night of icy cold in the drafty bunks, their stiff, skinny bodies hardly withstood the driving gusts of wind that buffeted them as they stood in straight lines in front of their barracks. Resisting the wind required more strength than many of the frozen, malnourished inmates could muster. Every morning some prisoners missed roll call. Their stiff corpses, frozen during the night, were found in their bunks.

The work teams still went out every day. Elie was on a

team which moved bricks. At times, he found his fingers fused to the ice-cold bricks.

Disease devastated the camp during winter. As they grew weaker, the men at Buna worried constantly about the selection, knowing well that they were of no use should they become ill and incapable of working. Some among them became what in camp slang were called *Muselmänner*—defeated, weary bodies, shuffling through the day, expressionless, without vestige of hope. Once the SS discovered the presence of such inmates, they were usually victims of the next selection.

Soon after the start of the year 1945, Elie noticed that the extreme cold had swollen his foot to double its size. The pain was so intense that he could not step on the foot. Reluctantly, he went to have it examined. The camp doctor had once been a famous Jewish surgeon, now he was a prisoner at Buna. He ordered Elie into the camp hospital and told him he needed an operation.

The hospital was only another barracks like Block 36—his own—but Elie found that life in the hospital was just a little bit easier. He was lying on a white sheet, received a thicker soup, and did not have to abide by the bell which regulated their daily lives, nor did he have to stand for interminable roll calls. Best of all, he had kind words from the doctor, whom he liked instantly, even when the medical verdict was unpleasant. Elie needed immediate surgery. Waiting might cost him his toes, even the whole leg. Elie's first thought was: "How will my father manage?"

The hospital barracks had a room used for surgery. There Elie was taken one morning to have his operation. The surgeon had few instruments; no anesthesia was available for inmates. Elie knew it was going to hurt, but the doctor said he would have to be courageous. He tried his best. Sometime during the hour-long operation, he fainted.

When Elie awoke, his immediate frantic thought was that his leg had been amputated. But his trust in the kind surgeon was justified. The doctor assured him that he had not taken off any limbs but had only drained the foot of a severe infection. In two weeks, Elie would walk again.

While he lay in bed, rumors flew through the hospital that Russian troops were nearby and would soon liberate the camp. Rumors were always part of the daily camp routine. This time, though, there were sounds of actual gunfire. In the darkness, Elie saw red flashes light up the frosted window panes of the hospital. Perhaps there was something to the rumors after all.

Two days later, the camp received orders to evacuate. Elie, lying in bed, waiting for his foot to heal, considered the alternatives. How could he march with the others in his present state? Did he dare stay behind in the hospital and risk being killed by the SS before they departed from the camp? It was not likely that the Germans would leave any patients behind to be liberated by the Russians.

Elie could not fit a shoe over his bandaged foot. The gauze covering the wound was soaked in blood. Blood even seeped through the strips of blanket he wrapped around his throbbing foot. His every step left a red mark in the snow. Yet, Elie decided to evacuate camp, along with his father. It was the one thing they could do to save their lives.

The journey on foot from Buna to Buchenwald became an exercise in human cruelty and the extremes of nature. During the ten days it took, Elie was in such pain from his wound that dying in the ice and snow seemed easier than having to go on. The pain, the exhaustion, the hunger, and the bitter, biting wind were more than he thought he could endure. Seeing men shot by the SS because they could no longer walk, looking on as others were trampled underfoot by the silent weary mass of marchers, Elie almost envied the dead. They did not have to walk any more.

Shlomo stayed at his side, pulling Elie on when he faltered, keeping him awake when they rested in the deadly snow and Elie faded into sleep. Staying alive for his father's sake was Elie's only reason for not giving up. What would they do without each other?

Despite his daze and pain, Elie witnessed a drama which touched him deeply. In his group were an old rabbi from Poland and his son. They had been Elie's fellow inmates since their arrival in Auschwitz. Just as Shlomo and Elie were inseparable, so had Rabbi Eliahou and his son taken care of each other from the very beginning, sharing all and sustaining one another. They, too, had kept each other alive through mutual devotion. During the march from Buna, they were separated. Elie saw the old father searching for his only, beloved son.

When Rabbi Eliahou came to him during a stop in the march, asking whether he had seen his son, Elie was too weary to collect his thoughts. He could not then remember that he had, indeed, seen the rabbi's son. And that the son, observing how his father struggled in the snow, growing weaker and slower with each step, had walked on without him. The son suddenly wanted to be rid of his father, deliberately. He was abandoning him to his sure fate. The burden had become too much. Now he had to look out for himself!

Elie did not tell the old rabbi that he had seen his son. When he remembered the episode afterwards, he was glad he had not robbed the father of the illusion that his son was searching for him too. But Elie was very troubled, even though his soul was as numb as his body.

And, in spite of myself, a prayer rose in my heart,
to that God in whom I no longer believed.

My God, Lord of the Universe, give me
strength never to do what Rabbi Eliahou's son has
done.

(Night)

But Elie, too, was not to be spared, though he fought such
debasing thoughts.

The final stage of their trip to Buchenwald was made in
open boxcars. The cars were large enough for possibly
forty men, but one hundred emaciated skeletons were
pushed into each one by the SS. Frozen in a standing
position, they leaned against each other for support. Each
man who fell was certain to be trampled underfoot
immediately.

They had had no nourishment for days. The bread
rations they had brought along from the last camp were
soon exhausted. As they stood in the heavily-falling snow,
some of the men managed to scrape some frozen snow
from the shoulders of men in front of them, eating it with
the spoons they had brought with them. This sight
produced merriment from the SS troops who observed it.
Elie never forgot their laughter.

During the ride, Elie noticed that Shlomo's eyes were
closed. When his father did not respond to his voice, Elie
was certain he was dead. And his first reaction was the
thought that now he himself was finished too. What use
was there in continuing the struggle? Without his father
to care for, he could finally give up.

The train stopped. The SS men alongside the cars
yelled that all the dead should be thrown out while there
was time. Inside, the more vigorous wanted room to
breathe and stretch. Asleep in a stupor, Elie came to just

in time to see two men approaching his father, ready to toss him overboard with the other corpses. Frantically Elie threw himself on his father and slapped his face as hard as he could. He was desperate in his attempts to hold off the men who wanted to get rid of Shlomo.

Hysterically he yelled out that his father was alive: he had seen Shlomo's eyelids move and had noticed his faint breathing. Saved one more time. The two scavengers, who removed the clothing from each body before they pitched it out, tackled their next prey. Elie collapsed from relief and weakness. The corpses were left behind, naked, in the deep snows of Poland.

The feeling Elie had dreaded came to him, too, shortly after they finally arrived in Buchenwald. Their arrival coincided with an air raid alert at the camp. In the scramble and the darkness, Elie became separated from his father. When the alert was over, Elie was so utterly exhausted that he fell asleep right where he was, on the wooden plank of a bunk bed. When he awoke the next morning, his first thought was of Shlomo. Where was his father?

> I went to look for him.
>
> But at the same moment this thought came into my mind: "Don't let me find him! If only I could get rid of this dead weight, so that I could use all my strength to struggle for my own survival, and only worry about myself." Immediately I felt ashamed of myself, ashamed forever.
>
> *(Night)*

Now Elie was like the old rabbi's son after all. The desperation of the moment had been too much for him. The guilt left behind by the fleeting wish became a heavy burden.

When he found Shlomo soon afterwards, Elie determined not to leave his side again unless forced to do so by camp routine. During the next few days, when Shlomo became deathly ill, growing steadily weaker from the dysentery which was consuming him, Elie used his own bread ration to bribe the man who slept in the bunk above Shlomo to trade quarters with him. Now he was with his father all night and as much during the day as he could manage. He could do little else for him. Though Elie gave Shlomo his own rations of bread and soup, his father slipped away a little more each day. Elie could see that this time there would be no miracle. Shlomo was changing before his eyes. But there were still other torments to be overcome. Shlomo complained of being beaten by his bunkmates. When Elie had to be out of the barracks, Shlomo was hit by the others, who resented his eating the bit of bread which might be keeping them alive a little longer. The worst for Elie was to see his father hit by the truncheon of an SS man while moaning and calling out in his delirium. To be so helpless at such a time of heartbreak!

This was to be Elie's last image of his father—cruelly beaten and abused during his last hours on earth. When Elie awoke in the darkness of dawn on January 29, 1945, someone new occupied the bunk below him. He had not even known his father's moment of death. Perhaps his father was still alive when he was taken away. Elie was never to know.

What was worse, as a pious Jewish son Elie could not even pray over his father. The ritual of death: human remains, a grave, a funeral; none of the ceremonials with which the living honor the dead and heal their own grief . . . none of these were available to Elie. He was even denied the final tribute to Shlomo: he could not cry.

12

In the days after his father's death, Elie was moved to the children's block. Like every other barracks at Buchenwald, this long wooden building held tiers and tiers of planks on which prisoners slept, one thousand per building. Only a few hundred children remained in the camp when Elie was transferred to their section. The survivors were adolescents, aged ten to seventeen. Most of them had lied about their true age when they first arrived at a concentration camp; by appearing older they had managed to become part of a labor squad. The younger children, too weak for work, were weeded out immediately. At the initial selection in Birkenau, they were ordered to the right, into the lines which led to the gas chambers. Some of the youngsters, like Elie, had succeeded in staying close to a relative and became part of his daily routine. When the relative died, the surviving child was moved.

The block leaders in charge of the children were not quite as severe and strict as the kapos in the adult barracks, who were ever ready to enforce discipline with their truncheons. Also, Elie discovered when he was moved into the children's block, he did not have to work.

Now he lay on his bunk for hours in a dazed stupor, staring into space. He was too weak to feel bored. The roll call twice daily and the line-up for the distribution of bread and soup consumed all his strength. Apathetic and weary, Elie drifted through the days as in a dream. He was no longer troubled by thoughts of his family; it was as if they had never existed. He floated in a void, without memories, interrupted only by dreams of food. Even here, in the children's barracks, rumors of approaching Allied troops reached his ears. Elie was too tired to pay them attention. He knew he would never get out of the camp alive. Even if Buchenwald were liberated, its inmates would not see freedom. The SS would not allow their prisoners to remain alive that long.

It was always easy to tell when the war was going badly for Germany: each air raid by the Allies, each retreat by the Wehrmacht brought more harsh treatment upon the camp inmates as their SS guards grew more murderous. During the first days of April, aware that he had already spent a year in captivity, Elie realized that the tempo of daily life in Buchenwald was plunging into turmoil and disarray.

"The SS is evacuating Buchenwald," one of Elie's friends muttered while the boys were sweeping the barracks.

It was easy to sense that something was about to change. The tense prisoners, noting the chaotic mood of their guards, feared that change.

When Elie dragged himself to roll call in front of the block in early daylight, he spotted the inmates of other blocks being ordered into columns of five and marched toward the camp gate. These groups were too large for work details. He noticed that none of the marchers carried picks, shovels, or other labor-squad paraphernalia.

Lined up again, for evening name check, Elie saw that many of the nearby barracks were empty. The inmates he had watched that morning had not returned.

The camp was emptying out; every day another thousand men were marched off. From the way the Germans swooped through the compound, rounding up prisoners for "evacuation," it wouldn't be long before the Allies arrived. If only the inmates could hold out that long!

Among themselves, the youngsters breathed rumors that their "chief," the Czech Christian prisoner in charge of the children's block, had managed to alter the records, so their names would not appear on the lists used by the SS to "clean up" the camp. Elie heard whispers that the camp resistance was awaiting the proper moment to surface.

He knew of the internal government which existed among the inmates. Among the older prisoners, especially the political prisoners incarcerated in Buchenwald for a number of years, were leaders whose word ruled the other inmates. The block elders were part of this group. They received their orders directly from the SS and were responsible for assigning and carrying out all tasks. Elie assumed that among the leaders of this hierarchy must be members of the resistance. So far, none of them had revealed themselves.

Camp life seemed to continue, to judge by the regularity of the roll calls. Until one evening when the children's block stood outside its building, waiting in vain for an SS officer to appear and check them off his list. They stood for two hours, waiting, not daring to break their ranks.

Finally, encouraged by the falling darkness, and the fact that they were apparently forgotten, the youngsters crept into their barracks, one by one. Suddenly the camp loudspeaker made them jump:

"All Jews report to the assembly place immediately!"

This was bad news. Everyone knew it. Dared they disobey? The raised arm of the block kapo, bringing his policeman's club down on the skull of any loiterer, decided their choice. Slowly, they made their way to the gathering spot.

"Get back. Go back to the block and stay put!" Voices hissed at the youngsters in the darkness. "Don't leave your barracks or you will be shot by the Germans."

Quickly, they used the noise and general confusion of another loudspeaker announcement as cover for their return to their block. The roll call at the assembly place had been called off for this evening. It would take place the following day. For tonight, the resistance had saved them.

When they did assemble the next day, the inmates were told that no further food supplies would be distributed. The camp was being evacuated. When the last person had left, Buchenwald was to be blown up.

Some six hundred children lay on the floor of the barracks, not daring to raise their heads. Outside the block, feverish activity and the sound of guns kept them from venturing out. They were mad with hunger, for it had now been six days since the Germans stopped giving out food. Some of the more desperate kids crept on hands and feet toward the kitchen where, in unemptied garbage pails, they found some potato peels which they ate raw. Others, less daring, chewed on blades of grass which grew near the back steps of the barracks.

The last mass assembly took place on April 10. The SS was still moving out blocks of prisoners, one after another. The rest of the inmates remained standing in the large assembly field, waiting to be evacuated. They had been told that by nightfall the camp would be empty. The wailing of air raid sirens interrupted the evacuation. Once again, the falling of darkness prevented the Germans from carrying out their plan of total evacuation.

The children returned to their barracks. Early the next

morning the resistance group opened fire on the retreating camp administration, using the weapons they had
hidden away for such a long time. Guns and grenades
thundered for a few hours, then the camp became eerily
quiet. Soon the resistance group took over the camp
leadership.

On April 11, 1945, American armed forces liberated the
concentration camp at Buchenwald. The soldiers who
entered the camp gates stared in disbelief at twenty
thousand living skeletons, among which were several
hundred children.

"Food poisoning," pronounced the military physician of
the U.S. Third Army after examining Elie, who had been
brought into the former SS hospital at Buchenwald, taken
over by the army immediately after the liberation. The
boy was in a coma and running a high fever. The doctor
had seen so many such cases during the first few days that
he was able to diagnose Elie's illness with ease. The
survivors all had tried to gobble up great amounts of food
right after the army entered Buchenwald: some of them
had died as a result. The physician shook his head at the
ignorance of the crews manning the field kitchens. They
had handed out foods too rich in protein and fat to the
surviving camp inmates; the digestive systems of these
starving people, deprived for too long, had simply re-
belled. The GI's meant well; the individual soldiers were
still sharing their rations with anyone they could. Just
looking at these poor souls made them feel guilty that they
were eating.

Elie awoke from his coma in the army hospital, on a clean
bed with white sheets, and did not know what was

happening to him. He called for his mother over and over again. He believed they were all together again, and that she would put her cool hand on his forehead and make him feel better.

When the fever went down, he was too weak to get up. For many days army nurses fed him, military doctors examined him and prescribed medications. Elie realized that he was very sick. Even now, he was sure he would die. How absurd it was to have survived all the camps only to die after the liberation, he thought. But he didn't die . . .

When Elie felt a little better, he remembered the piece of ham. It was the last thing he remembered about being liberated. First, after the Germans fled Buchenwald, there was the raid on the provisions. Someone had found the store of bread left behind in the camp kitchen and had tossed loaves through the window to his waiting friends on the outside. Elie's only thoughts had been about food. He stuffed himself full of bread; eating proved to him that he was alive. When the Americans brought food into camp, Elie was given a piece of ham. He had been brought up religiously; ordinarily he would not have eaten pork. During his time of captivity, he would probably have been glad to eat it, to eat anything at all. After liberation, Elie took one bite of the ham, and fainted.

When it was time to discharge Elie from the hospital, American army officers came to talk with him. They spoke to him of his future. Elie looked at them, his eyes dull, uncomprehending. He was still too weak to think. Now that he was suddenly given a future, he had no strength to plan for it. He knew he had survived, somehow, but what lay beyond he could not imagine. All the words drifted past him, vague and hazy. He knew he had never been so alone before. Not one member of his family was left. He had lost his whole world. He was *alone*.

"Would you like to go home?"

The American officer interviewing Elie was obviously a kind, well-meaning man. He had a job to do, but Elie wondered whether the man really understood.

Home to Sighet? It seemed such a strange thought. Sighet without his father, without his mother's Shabbat candles, without Dodye's songs?

The American thumbed through the lists of survivors. Elie checked them very carefully for the names of his two older sisters. Perhaps they had survived and returned to their home? He found their names nowhere on the sheets the officer showed him.

At the very end Shlomo, in his pain and delirium, had whispered to Elie that he had buried some money in the cellar of their house. And Elie, to ease his father's mind, told him not to worry. Someday they would go back together to look for the hidden goods they had left behind.

Elie remembered Sighet as he had seen it that last Sunday in the sunshine, while the human snake wound its way around the town square on its way to the railroad station. That Sighet was now *judenrein*, devoid of Jews, just as its inhabitants had wanted it to be.

"I have no home," he said to the kind American officer, who shook his head gently, as if to say, "Doesn't everyone want to go home?"

Elie said no more. He did not wish to offend the nice American.

Part II

Part II

13

Few of the children noticed that the train had stopped. They had traveled for two days this cold April of 1945, rolling through the bleak German country-side aboard the train the U.S. Army had requisitioned for them. They had boarded the train at the camp, four hundred grotesquely emaciated boys, aged ten through seventeen, the remaining survivors of the children's block at Buchenwald. Their American military escort was evacuating them from Germany.

In his seat by the window, Elie awoke shivering. He wondered how long the train had been sitting still. Were they already in Belgium?

A cold draft seeped through the cracks in the window frame. Elie fastened the buttons of his new jacket, which hung loosely on him. He turned to see whether anyone else was awake. Wherever he looked, his companions were slouched in sleep.

For the kids on this train, the war was over, even though the official document of surrender had not yet been signed by the German High Command. Few of the children bothered to look out of the windows, once they had climbed aboard. For them, there was little reason to watch the houses, telephone poles, and German road signs slipping past. The faster they got out of Germany, the better. They sat quietly in their seats with little baggage, except for the new clothing they had received in

101

exchange for the striped prison garb. They were totally fatigued from weakness and exhaustion. Relieved to be moving, they leaned back into the upholstered seats and soon fell asleep. Their shaved heads, sprouting new hair, nodded in the rhythm of the train wheels.

Elie, too, had dozed often while the train trundled through Germany, jolted by every broken track along the way. Now he became alert when the wheels stopped, and he tried to squint through the window. The residue of wartime camouflage paint and decades of railroad soot had settled on the glass, yet Elie made out that they were sitting on a siding. In the thin April sunshine, there was no sign of a train station. On a platform between railroad tracks, several of the Americans accompanying this transport stood talking to the train personnel. Elie saw the train's engineer making sweeping arm movements. The man stabbed his finger repeatedly at a piece of paper in his other hand. From his irate gestures, it appeared that the engineer was excited.

Elie was bone-tired. He did not care whether they arrived in Belgium sooner or later. If that was where they were going, it made little difference to him when they got there. It was good to know that Belgium wanted them. But the truth was, he was very disappointed.

After the war, the British government had closed the door to Palestine, refusing all entrance to Jewish immigration. Often, during his camp days, Elie had tried to imagine the joy of being free and had looked forward to the new life he would have in Eretz Yisrael. Now that time was here. He was not elated. Instead a heavy weight lay around his heart.

"Do you think they'll put us into another camp?" asked the boy sitting next to Elie. His name was Ancek, and Elie knew him from Sighet. Ancek, too, was an orphan now. He had spoken little during the trip, dozing most of the time. Awake now, Ancek was afraid that they might be near their destination. His sunken eyes looked troubled.

"How will we understand them?" he wanted to know. "We don't speak French, and that's the language in Belgium. What will we do?"

Ancek reached into the brown paper bag he kept close to his body and retrieved a forgotten cookie. For a few moments the cookie provided contented nibbling.

Elie had touched none of the food they were given by the social workers who had helped with the train boarding. Stabbing pains still cut into his gut every time he ate. He ended up vomiting the food his stomach had forgotten how to digest. It was better not to eat at all.

Suddenly the train lurched, then resumed its forward motion. A noise at the front of the car alerted all to face in that direction. Even the last sleeper awoke in time to see the heavy door open. Through it stepped their American officer guard, followed by his interpreter.

"Attention everybody," the interpreter called out. "The lieutenant has an announcement to make."

Every youngster in the car stared in total silence at the American, who told them there had been a change in their travel plans. They were not going to Belgium. A special order had come from the French commander, General Charles DeGaulle, and this transport was now heading toward Paris. They would live in France from now on.

The fields of France were neatly parceled out. Planted and fertile, they were ready to bloom in the early spring. As the train moved through the plains, Elie saw a little girl, ribbons in her pigtails, standing close to a couple guiding a horse-drawn plow. The child lifted her arm and waved to the passing train. Her face wore a big smile. What a lucky little girl to have her family, to want to smile at a train filled with strangers. Elie tried to remember the last time someone had smiled at him. He thought of the blank faces staring with indifference at the prisoners as their open truck moved through German villages. The little girl must be about seven years old, like Tzipora. Last year, in April, the Wiesels had all been together in Sighet.

It was late afternoon when they approached Paris. The city's very name had an exciting ring. Aboard the train the chatter grew more lively. Some of the boys remembered things they had heard about Paris; others speculated on the life they would lead in France. Some had relations there for whom they would search.

Elie, too, thought about his future. It was all very confusing. Only two days before, at a loading platform in Germany, he had left the past behind. He was sixteen years old and not yet used to the idea that he even *had* a future. Now that they were almost in Paris he was worried. How would he live, how would he manage, all alone? His friend Ancek was right: he didn't know the language.

Elie knew *what* he must do. That he had sensed on the day they had allowed him to get up at the army hospital and he had looked at himself in a mirror. It was the first time he had seen his reflection since leaving home. He had hardly recognized himself. He knew then that he must testify to the events which had changed a boy into a survivor. It was his duty to be a witness. If there was a meaning to the unbelievable experience behind him, he had to find it and let others know. But how could he express what he had seen?

As a youngster, Elie had planned that he would write someday. While still secure in his life in Sighet, he had written a book of commentaries on the Bible, and he had thought, then, that he would write other religious books in the years to come.

But now he knew that his writings would have to tell a different tale. *How* to do it, troubled him. What words does one use to describe the unspeakable?

He would not speak until he was ready. To get ready, he must study. How else could he understand what had happened to him? He would study languages, sharpen the skills of communication. When he knew the right words, he could paint the world he had known and lost on his way to hell. Only when he understood why they were no longer with him would he speak of those whose lives he had shared.

It might take as long as ten years to prepare himself. Until then, he would not break his vow of silence.

For the first time, Elie believed his life had been spared for a reason.

14

Wʜᴇɴ ᴇʟɪᴇ's ᴛʀᴀɪɴ rolled into the smog-filled French railroad depot, it was met by journalists and photographers, and by ladies whose armbands identified them as members of the Jewish children's-aid group, the Oeuvre de Secour aux Enfants, known as OSE. The OSE had been requested by the French government to care for the newly-arrived camp survivors brought into France. The bewildered children stood around in the smoky hall, giving their names to the OSE social workers, trying to answer questions from the press asked through interpreters. When the registration formalities were completed at the railroad station, another train whisked the children away to a vacation home near the town of Ecouis in Normandy, where a former castle had been converted to house and rehabilitate them.

Among the well-manicured grounds and flower-bordered paths in Ecouis, the forlorn survivors of Buchenwald's children's block felt miserable. They walked around the estate where aristocracy had once cavorted and were aware of how alone they were. Even the kindness of the staff did not help. With each day spent at Ecouis, their dream of rejoining a loved one who might have also survived, faded a little more. They felt lost, unhappy.

No one understood them in this new country whose

language they did not speak. Even in the dining hall they huddled in little groups because they had trouble talking to the kitchen help. Appreciatively, they ate the good food served them. The excellent milk and cheeses, the splendid fruit of the Normandy countryside nourished their starved bodies. They hoped it would not be long before they regained the normal weight of teenagers.

It was difficult to believe that they were close to a former war zone where bitter battles had followed the D-Day landings less than a year before, and where prized Normandy farmland had been uprooted and destroyed.

Sunbathing in the genial temperatures of the Normandy spring, his hair tousled by warm breezes, Elie tried to forget the eternal cold which had become a part of his body. He craved the warmth of which he had been deprived for so long. When he became restless, he walked through the grounds and circled the edges of the camp, where the estate met the tall trees of the neighboring forests.

During his walks, Elie tried to envision what his life would be like from now on. What would he do, alone, without the advice and guidance he had always received from parents and teachers? He would continue his schooling, that appealed to him the most. If all else was lost, the world of books still remained. He missed the studies which had been interrupted in Sighet. He decided to see the head of the children's home and ask him for some books so he could continue the study of Talmud.

In Paris, a newly-married young woman, recently liberated from Auschwitz, opened the pages of the evening newspaper. Her French was not too good yet, and it helped to read the papers, to see words in print. Suddenly the young woman screamed. She ran to her husband, a young Algerian with whom she had emigrated to France.

"It's Leizer. Look, look," she shouted. Her finger pointed to a photograph in the newspaper. She was too excited to talk; tears ran down her cheeks. Her husband took the paper from her, guiding his wife, Hilda, to a chair, and together they studied the picture and its accompanying story of a group of children, saved from the concentration camp in Buchenwald, who had been brought to France, where they were now recuperating at a rest home in Normandy.

The couple's immediate reaction was to go to the nearest post office, purchase the necessary token for the telephone, and call long-distance to the home mentioned in the newspaper story.

Once he had made up his mind to continue with his Jewish studies, Elie visited the director of the vacation home, Monsieur Wolff, to ask for some books he would need. While he was in his office, the director received a telephone call. Elie thought he heard his name mentioned, but since Monsieur Wolff spoke in French, Elie had no idea what he was saying and was too polite to ask. As the director hung up the receiver, he turned back to Elie.

"Your sister just called from Paris."

Elie was stunned. He tried to convince the director there must be an error. His sisters were no longer alive. He knew, because he had checked the survivor lists before leaving camp; his sisters' names had not appeared on them. If his sisters had survived, why had they not gone back to Sighet? Why would they be in France? How did anyone know he was here, in this place?

Elie poured out all these questions to the patient Monsieur Wolff, because he wanted to protect himself against a major shock. Suppose this was not his family?

All Monsieur could tell him was the message the woman on the telephone had given him.

"Your sister said to take the morning train to Paris tomorrow. She will meet you at Gare Saint-Lazare."

Passing time until his Paris arrival the next day was more than Elie thought he could stand. Would his sister really be at the other end? Twisting and turning in bed that night, he worried that he would meet the wrong person. Perhaps a stranger would turn up at the station; perhaps it was all a bad mistake.

There was only one morning train to Paris from Ecouis. When Elie stepped down from the compartment steps, a young woman ran toward him, enfolded him in her arms, and cried tears of joy over him. It was his older sister, Hilda.

Hilda had an amazing story to tell. Both she and Beatrice, the middle sister, had remained together in the same camp. Both had survived. Hilda had met her young man after liberation; he was a former inmate of the same concentration camp. Shortly afterwards, they married and came to France. Beatrice, however, had returned to Sighet to look for Elie. From some of the other returned camp survivors who knew the Wiesel family, she had heard reports that Elie had died. While Bea was still in Sighet, Hilda had opened the newspaper in Paris, and there, in front of her eyes was Elie's picture . . .

After such a miraculous reunion, it was difficult to separate again. But Hilda and her husband were desperately poor. They had one room and a bare subsistence for themselves. Elie, on the other hand, was being supported by the OSE. It would be unwise to cut him off from this aid, as long as they had no money to keep him with them in Paris. For the present, he would stay in the care of the agency. After only one day with his sister, Elie returned to the castle in Normandy. It was a painful decision, but he was sustained by the knowledge that both Hilda and Bea were alive and that he now had hopes of seeing both again in the future.

When the youngsters in Elie's group had first been received by the children's agency, they were divided into two sections: those to whom kosher food and a religious upbringing were important, and those to whom this did not matter.

Despite his feelings of rebellion during the camp experience, Elie wanted to stay with the religious group. His entire upbringing had been religious. He felt he owed it to his family to observe the tenets of Judaism, more than ever now that all of them were gone and he remained the only male to carry on their tradition. If anything was clear to Elie during these hazy days of readjustment, it was that he must always be Jewish and observant.

The first four weeks in France passed. Those of the youngsters who had opted to remain observant and needed kosher food were sent to another part of France. The agency taking care of refugee children acquired a number of châteaux which were ideally suited to the purpose of sheltering groups of youngsters and keeping them isolated until they had gotten used to the language and customs of their new country.

In the château near the town of Amblois, Elie began learning French, in silence. He listened when others spoke: the director of the home, its employees, its visitors. He looked up new words in a pocket dictionary which he carried on his person.

Elie graduated to the next château, coming closer to Paris, when he was sent to live in Taverny, where there were many young people who, like him, were religious and spent much of their time studying, hoping that someday they might be permitted to emigrate to Palestine. Elie gave Hebrew lessons to some of the younger refugees. He studied Talmud in the company of some of the boys his age. But mainly he tried to read. Sitting on the lawn, propped against one of the tall shade trees abounding on the château property, he read whatever literature was provided for the agency's wards.

Eager for higher learning, Elie hoped someday to attend the Sorbonne in Paris and take courses in philosophy. Perhaps this would help him to gain a new perspective. He needed to sort out what had happened to him, so that he might understand more about the relationship between man and his universe.

When the steady rains of autumn came and forced everyone indoors, Elie continued his studies, near a fireplace in the huge, chilly hall of the château, where he felt warmer and less confined than in the tiny dormitory room he shared with others.

Learning the French language meant a new life, a new home to Elie. Along with the haven he found in France, its language meant new beginnings, new worlds, to him.

When he was moved to yet another château, this one in Versailles, only forty minutes from Paris, Elie felt that he was almost near his goal. His next stop would be the capital city.

While Elie was at Versailles, a young man named François Wahl came to the château. François was not Jewish, but he knew that young people who had survived the Nazi camps were housed there and wanted to help in whatever way he could.

Someone introduced François to Elie. When Elie learned that François was a graduate student of philosophy at the Sorbonne, he told him, in halting beginner's French, that he too wanted to study philosophy someday.

François became interested in the youngster and offered to tutor him. He suggested to Elie that the two of them could read some French classics together. Though this was an unusual way to learn the language, Elie gratefully accepted the offer.

From then on, Elie and François Wahl read aloud from works that were the glory of French literature. They began with a play by Racine, a seventeenth-century dramatist: perfection at the highest level. They analyzed the contents of that play and others. Analyzing a text was a familiar process for Elie, who had received a firm grounding in the technique of text analysis during his early talmudic studies. It seemed to work fine with French classics too.

From time to time, Elie's young teacher left other books for him to read, works of other cultures, but written in French. In gratitude for his newly gained knowledge of the French classics, Elie taught François Wahl some of the principles of Judaism.

As the weeks in Versailles drew to a close, Elie knew that soon he would be on his own. Away from the others, some of whom had shared his destiny and his domicile, he would have to take care of himself in Paris, living and working by his own wits. It was yet another challenge to be faced, perhaps the most difficult yet.

15

From the porte de saint cloud, in the 16th *arrondissement* of Paris, a network of narrow crowded streets fans outward into a typical working-class quarter. In one of these gray, anonymous streets, the Rue de Marois, in a tiny room without running water, containing only a bed, one chair, and a small table, Elie began life in the French capital in 1946.

The OSE found him the room and provided the small stipend which covered the monthly rent of ten dollars and, if he managed well, one meal a day. As a foreigner, he was not allowed to work. He was eighteen, a stateless nobody, and penniless. The only document he had to prove his identity was a residence permit which, as an alien, he had to renew periodically at the Paris Prefecture of Police.

Except for his older sister, who had her own problems of keeping body and soul going, Elie knew hardly anyone in Paris. It was of no great consequence to anyone that he was even alive. In bitter moments he felt that the Germans had not only taken his family and his hometown away from him, they had also swallowed his reason for living.

His landlady, and the other residents of his Paris tenement, avoided the undersized, silent young man whose eyes spoke of great sadness. Elie did not encourage

113

anyone to become friendly with him. He spoke to no one, had nobody who would visit him. The original members of his group were now scattered; some remained in France, others hoped for visas to the United States.

In the neighborhood bistro where Elie took his one meal a day, he ate his food with the single-minded determination to stay alive. He hated to eat alone, but he made no gesture to get acquainted with the other regulars who ate at the restaurant. He wanted no questions.

During those first few months of being alone in Paris, he felt guilty for having survived. During sleepless nights, he envied the dead their deaths; they no longer had to fight their way through life, their pain was behind them. His would endure the rest of his days.

Elie was troubled that he had emerged from the living hell of the camps, while others, perhaps far worthier, had not. Had his life been bought at the expense of someone else's death? He could see no meaning in the experiences he had been through. Nothing would ever explain the random, casual system by which men, women, and children had gone to their grotesque deaths. Neither wealth nor poverty, education nor simplicity, faith nor doubt had seemingly influenced their destiny.

In his cramped little room, Elie sat on his bed, brooding. He wondered why he had survived, questioned whether there was any purpose to his life. When the walls pushed in on him, he left his room for long walks. He explored Paris thoroughly, by day and by night. He investigated most of the neighborhoods which made up the city, and found that walking relieved his pain. He strolled along the Seine and became acquainted with the quais on either side of the great river. He looked at the wares of the booksellers but could not afford any purchases. He read on benches of little neighborhood parks and watched the habitués who frequented them, old men, and women pushing their infants in carriages. He visited the city's famous museums and studied their masterpieces. Nothing unburdened his soul of the evil it had witnessed.

Elie pushed out all thoughts of his lost family. He refused entry to memories of his mother, father, grandfather, little sister. He knew that giving in to the huge, consuming grief inside him would destroy him. He discussed his thoughts with no one and had no means of giving shape to his pain.

Meanwhile, he was hungry most of the time. The luxury of which he dreamed these days was a visit to the local cafe where he might order coffee with real milk. When the agency stipend ended, Elie wondered where he would find work, any kind, to sustain himself. He could do with very little food, but he needed to pay the rent.

In his walks around the neighborhood, Elie discovered a number of synagogues in the area of Montmartre. He learned that one of these synagogues was heavily attended by refugees, and he decided to go there. Perhaps he would be able to get some advice or a recommendation to help him find a job.

It was the first time Elie had been to a synagogue since Sighet, and he was pained to find so few worshippers at the Friday night service. He remembered the piety and fervor of his grandfather's favorite prayer hall. The few men in the large Paris synagogue chatted about politics, prices, external events. He felt a total outsider, but he kept in mind his reason for coming here this night.

After services, Elie engaged one of the men in conversation and asked him about the prospects for work.

"I am willing to do any kind of job," Elie said. "I need to work to stay alive."

In reply, he received a lecture on the difficulty of life in France during this postwar period, on the nearly impossible working conditions the native Frenchman was suffering just now.

"Do you know what obstacles you are facing, young man? You are not a French citizen, you don't know very much French, you are living on a visitor's visa. You are not even supposed to work, according to government regulations which prohibit foreigners from working in France."

Having delivered himself of this wordy lecture, the man was moved to direct Elie to an organization he knew of that might be able to help.

The following week, Elie visited the agency. He was kept in its offices for a three-hour interrogation. It seemed to please the agency worker to question Elie pointedly.

"How long do you intend to live in Paris at someone else's expense?"

Elie was so humiliated and angry that he found it difficult to restrain himself. There was no use yelling, not even to explain that the situation in which he found himself was not of his making. Why waste his precious strength to fight with such an unlikely adversary as the interviewer?

Elie left the refugee organization with a sum of money that day. With it, he paid his astonished landlady the rent for several months in advance. Then he headed for one of the pedestrian bridges crossing the Seine to the Left Bank and completed the act of which he had dreamed for months: he registered as a student at the Sorbonne.

It was ironic that his great desire for learning was diluted by another, currently more urgent, motivation. Elie had discovered that as a student, with a student's permit, he would be allowed to work. At the moment, this was nearly as important to him as his studies.

As a student at the world-famous university located in the Latin Quarter of Paris, Elie sat in enormous lecture halls and heard distinguished professors speak on the subjects which had the deepest interest for him: literature, philosophy, and psychology.

Unlike many of his fellow students, who devoted more time to extracurricular activities like discussions, drinking, and student organizations than to attending lectures, Elie was intensely serious about his university studies. The courses he selected were all in disciplines that he needed to study: they helped him to understand himself and the world around him. They were his lifeline toward regaining the will to live.

An employment agency recommended that Elie teach Hebrew. He was sent to the homes of wealthy French families who could afford a tutor for their children. None of his jobs lasted long: Elie was too hard a teacher, and the children he tutored did not want to learn. He took his work seriously; he did not know that his students lacked the intense love of learning which had always driven him.

Elie accepted any position to which he was recommended; sometimes employment agencies sent him. He toiled over translations, taught Talmud, worked as a children's counselor in summer camps.

He never went back to the synagogue where many of the European refugees gathered.

Several times during his life, Elie has come to feel that few incidents happening to people are accidental. He prefers to think of them as encounters that were fated to take place.

When Elie started visiting a small synagogue on the Rue Pavé, near his room, he felt comfortable there, and so he returned to it frequently, seeking the peace of the

Sabbath in the company of congenial Friday night worshippers. He had been attending the sanctuary for many
weeks when, one Friday night, he met a strange, disturbing individual there.

> Always dirty, hairy, he looked like a hobo turned
> clown, or a clown playing hobo. He wore a tiny
> hat, always the same, on top of his immense round
> bloated head; his glasses, with their thick, dirty
> lenses, blurred his vision. Anyone encountering
> him on the street without knowing him would step
> out of his way with distaste. To his own great
> satisfaction, moreover.
>
> (*Legends of Our Time,*
> "The Wandering Jew")

When Elie saw him for the first time, this unusual old
man was explaining the Torah portion of the week to all
the other worshippers, who had gathered around to hear
him after prayers were concluded. Everything about the
speaker was displeasing to Elie that night: the man's
harsh, strident voice, his physical appearance, the aggressive, almost angry way in which he addressed the crowd
surrounding him. At the same time, Elie was fascinated
by the man's knowledge, which seemed awesome.

The man noticed the young stranger at once and
goaded him into a conversation. Elie was humiliated and
offended, but he was drawn to the old man. He had rarely
heard anyone speak so illuminatingly and brilliantly. Yet
the meeting ended badly. Elie's response, meant in
admiration, seemed to infuriate the old man, for he left
the synagogue in apparent violent anger.

The other worshippers consoled Elie. This was the
man's way, always angry and disagreeable, seeking out

victims among his audience to belittle. Tonight was not the first time he had acted so strangely.

Despite his consternation, Elie was excited by the meeting. He had not been so mentally stimulated since his master in Sighet had stirred his brain and soul. The old man had goaded Elie into asking questions on particular Bible passages and had answered every one of them in a dazzling fashion, defying Elie to ask more, increasingly difficult questions, none of which were too difficult for him.

For the first time since the camp, Elie felt interested in something, someone. His grief over the destruction of his world had numbed him, dulled him with pain. Suddenly this old man had shaken him up, hinting that he had answers to the questions that troubled him.

That Friday night, Elie wandered through the Paris streets for hours after leaving the synagogue. He must see that strange old man again. He knew he would become his student, follow him. Elie had no idea of the man's name, nor did he know his address. The Jews at the synagogue did not know either, but they assured Elie that the old man would return to the synagogue. He always did. Elie couldn't wait. He was too impatient to trust fate to bring about another meeting, which, he knew, would determine his future.

But he searched in vain that night and went home to his small room, discouraged. The old man did not return to the synagogue on the Rue Pavé, where Elie waited for him every Friday night.

In the meantime, both his Sorbonne courses and his working schedule kept Elie's days filled. He was doing some teaching of his own; twice a week he traveled to the Paris suburb of Taverny, where he lectured to a group of Hasidic refugee students, also charges of the OSE, who lived in one of the châteaux run by that organization.

Some months had passed since Elie's meeting with the old man. One day, he boarded his train at the Gare du Nord and settled down in his seat, hoping to use the hour-long trip as preparation time for the lecture ahead of him. While thumbing through his notes, Elie heard a voice calling him. Turning in the direction of the familiar-sounding tones, he saw the mysterious stranger.

Meeting him aboard the train was even more disturbing than the first encounter had been. The unusual events following this second meeting soon confirmed to Elie that his intuition had been right: it was fated that they should come together.

The old man followed Elie off the train and went with him to the château. With the most natural air of inevitability, he turned Elie's projected lecture into a shambles and took over the group of students. The young men were so fascinated by the intruder that they would not let him leave. Elie had prepared a single lecture for that day. Instead, the students listened to the old man night and day for a whole week. During that week, Elie, the teacher, was completely forgotten. He was, in fact, turned back into a student himself. Spellbound, he joined his class in listening as the old man accepted different topics from the students and wove them into a wreath of rhetoric which included every single question, fully answered, in one whole, complete lecture. The students were mesmerized by this dazzling display of knowledge. They had long forgotten the ugly old man's droll exterior, which had, at first, been cause for merriment. They also became oblivious of the passing of time and each day for a week sat huddled in amazed silence, hour after hour until midnight, while the Master discussed international politics, the atom bomb, the destruction of the Temple, the British mandate of Palestine, making them forget everything else, including their daily prayers.

Never before had Elie felt so humble. After this experience, he would no longer be able to teach this group of young men. He did not mind at all. The only thing that mattered was whether the old man would accept him as his disciple, once they returned to Paris.

So began the curious relationship between Elie and Rav Mordecai Shushani, whose name he did not learn until many years later, after his teacher had died. The relationship continued in the same strange manner in which it began.

Twice a week, Shushani came to Elie's bare little room. Elie never knew when to expect his Master, for the old man was completely oblivious to the passing of time, and to the needs for food and sleep. Shushani sat in the only chair the room had to offer, his student sat on the bed. Hours went by quickly; sometimes neither Master nor student noticed that day and night were turned around. Each time he turned up, the old man spoke on topics which interested him, weaving around them such an enormous wealth of knowledge that with each session Elie became more awed by the tremendous wisdom of his teacher.

During the time he knew him, Elie never learned the slightest clue about Rav Shushani. The old man clothed himself in mystery. Whenever Elie sought to question him about himself, his teacher's anger vented into such fury that Elie soon learned to keep their conversation totally impersonal.

While he was his student, Elie learned more from Rav Shushani than he would have believed possible. The old man's revelations were a priceless opportunity, and Elie was grateful for the time the Master gave him.

In May 1948, while Elie was still studying with the old man, the State of Israel came into life. His teacher discussed the birth of the new nation with him one night, at the same small synagogue where they had first met. Elie had gone to Friday night services excited and happy. To him, who had lost everything—his past, his world, his identity—the establishment of Israel was nothing less than a miracle. As he says, "Overnight I was robbed of even the smallest point of reference and support. I was confronted with emptiness. Everywhere. To avoid sinking, I needed a miracle, or at least a sign."

But his teacher disagreed.

"Call it miraculous, that I refuse. We have paid too dearly for it. To be a miracle, it would have had to happen a little sooner."

The connection between Master and disciple ended just as it had begun: suddenly, without warning. Elie bid his teacher goodbye one night at the Hôtel de Ville metro stop, to which he accompanied him after every session. Nothing indicated that it would be the last time. The Master never came to Elie's room again.

After seeing Rav Shushani regularly over a three-year period, Elie knew that the old man had mastered "thirty ancient and modern languages," memorized sacred Hindu writings as well as the Book of Splendor, and "felt at home in every culture, in every role." After the three years were over, Elie knew no more about his Master's life or background than he had learned after their first unusual meeting at the synagogue on the Rue Pavé.

16

ALL THE WHILE THAT ELIE, young and poor in Paris, was sharpening his mind on Rav Shushani's keen-witted teachings, he knew that outside the walls of his own, shabby room near the Hôtel de Ville, another world of exciting knowledge waited to be discovered by him. On the other side of the Seine, in the cafes and meeting places of Saint-Germain-des-Prés, on the Left Bank, new postwar philosophies, and their literary expressions, were under discussion. Elie had neither the money nor the time to be among the students and admirers who sat in the Deux Magots restaurant and the Cafe Flore to listen as their literary heroes expounded and exchanged ideas. During his Paris beginnings, he might not have had the language skills either.

But Elie caught up with the writings of the day in a hurry. In his classes on literature at the Sorbonne, he became exposed to new writers. He had never read novels and stories just for the pleasure of reading. His youthful education had not included fiction. Since he was so constantly occupied with religious texts which offered true, direct knowledge, there was no need for novels, which were, after all, only inventions. Elie's own intellectual curiosity soon changed his views.

One writer, in particular, touched Elie deeply. In future years, many people reading the works of Elie Wiesel would feel that his writings spoke to them personally, that his words were meant for them alone. Just so, Elie discovered in the writings of Albert Camus that he had found an author who mirrored his own feelings, a writer who expressed reactions which he, still an alien in the postwar world, could well appreciate. Elie found it intensely exciting to read Camus's novel *The Stranger* and, later, *The Plague*, and was warmed by Camus's love for humanity, by his compassion and great feeling for the individual man. Camus expressed intense respect for human life; for him, the totalitarian view of the world was anti-human. In a universe turned completely upside-down, when belief and direction had broken down, Camus showed in both his life and his writings that the commitment between people is important: friendship makes life worth living. For Elie, a victim of just such anti-human totalitarianism, Camus's views were comforting and inspiring.

Elie had been kept intensely occupied by his studies at the Sorbonne and his twice-weekly meetings with Rav Shushani. Now, without his Master, Elie felt alone again. Shushani had sustained him, had kept his mind so busy that he had forgotten the dreadful loneliness of those first days and nights in Paris. Now it returned, and with it, restlessness.

When, at the very moment of its birth, the new State of Israel was attacked and forced to fight before it had even begun life, Elie felt great urgency to be there. Having survived the Holocaust, he needed to be part of the struggle involving the new homeland, that soil longed for in the imagination and prayers of every pious Jew.

His immediate reaction was to volunteer for the army of the new country. Paris had a recruiting office, and there Elie was examined by an attending physician.

"I am afraid you are not strong enough to be accepted,"

said the doctor. "You should really be treated for the things that are wrong. Here is my card. Please come to see me at my private office."

Elie was not stopped by this discouragement. The urge within was greater than ever, and he had no intention of silencing it. Before long, he found a way to go to Israel.

The Israeli newspaper *Yediot Aharonot*, published in Tel Aviv, needed a Paris correspondent. For Elie, the timing could not have been better. The pay was small, but the articles he was to write were varied, and the training would be invaluable. He would serve an apprenticeship in the use of words, using the modern Hebrew language his father had once urged him to learn. Best of all, he could travel as much as he wanted: shipping companies and airlines rewarded the holder of a press card with free transportation.

Nothing held Elie in Paris. He had no home, few friends; his sisters did not need him. He was searching for answers, and he was restless. Roaming the world might not provide the answers he was seeking, but it would appease the restlessness. Elie's assignments were cabled to him from Tel Aviv, and he welcomed every one. His press card became the passport to new and strange places. He traveled to North Africa, South America, and India. He soon became a seasoned world traveler.

Early in 1949, Elie walked the streets of Jerusalem in time of war. It was his first trip to Israel. The other places he visited were segments of a long list of wanderings. They were the towns in which he tried to forget the one town which always pushed itself back into his mind: Sighet, his hometown. Yet one place drew him even more, a city of which he had dreamed long before he left Sighet. That city was Jerusalem.

Like every pious Jewish child, Elie knew what it was to yearn for the City of David. He learned it at his father's Passover table, the fervent wish at the conclusion of the Haggadah reading: "Next year in Jerusalem." He recalled Yom Kippur in Sighet and remembered the Hasidim, their fasting and praying done, wishing it for themselves, and for Jews everywhere: "Next year in Jerusalem."

Elie was haunted by the scene at their Shabbat table; his father and mother at odds on the Day of Rest. "Let us leave everything behind," she said. "Let us go to Palestine. Now, while there is still time." And his father's answer, "Nothing will happen here. No one will hurt us. We are living in the twentieth century."

How he, Elie, a well-mannered child, brought up to respect his parents' decisions, had urged his father to change his mind! And Shlomo, considering Elie a bit of a religious fanatic, had told him that he was free to go to Palestine if his heart was so inclined. But he would have to go alone. And Elie, so attached, so close to his family, could not bear the thought of leaving them.

And now he was here. Alone, after all.

Each stone reminded Elie that someone, everyone, in his childhood had at some time spoken of the wish to walk here one day. Jerusalem: the embodiment of their dreams, the hope of all he knew who had perished too soon.

He saw barbed wire, young soldiers and their guns, explosions, the fires. This was not the vision his Masters had seen. The City of Peace had changed its face. But it did not matter; someday her real face would return. Peace would come, and Jerusalem would again be the city of which exiles dreamed. Only then it would be no dream: it would be the home to which they could come.

Elie stayed less than two weeks that first time. Intense, restless, he is driven by the voices inside him. They are more actual to him than the outside voices which surround him. He tries to drown them in silence, but they won't let him be. They go where he goes, they run with him wherever he travels to get away from the past.

Deep inside him, he carried secrets which he confided to no living soul. No one heard him speak of the times and scenes he had seen while captive. Unlike other refugees, who spoke of nothing else, Elie never mentioned his experiences at all. Whatever seared him, still burned inside him, but it was his own private pain, he did not expose it to public view.

Driving his thoughts underground only increased the torment, but Elie held to his vow of silence. For him, silence was more meaningful than words. It was filled with memories, recollections, unbearable pain, but he was not yet ready to exchange that silence for words. He had not yet found adequate words.

During his travels, there were many weeks when Elie did not speak to anyone. Except for the functional conversations required of a traveler, total silence surrounded him. He imposed that silence upon himself; he needed it. It was a learning time.

In 1952, Elie was in India. He was on an assignment, but while there he started working on a dissertation comparing religious disciplines in the Hindu, Jewish, and Christian faiths. He was studying and writing; the manuscript grew rapidly. He decided to teach himself English, without any help. Again, he withdrew into silence. Just as he had done when learning French, he listened. He heard people speak English, and he let the sounds penetrate his ears. He began to read in English and encountered words he had heard in people's conversations. He had a gift for total recall. Without a teacher, and with a method he invented for himself, he "withdrew totally in silence and absorbed the language, just as one absorbs air or sounds." He emerged with a working knowledge of English.

Elie was a hard-working journalist. The newspaper articles, the reports he wrote from strange towns, from cafes, trains, at airports, were responses to the kind of reporting Israelis wanted from their overseas correspondents. At times, they concerned topics which hurt him personally.

In 1952, in Wassenaar, Holland, a suburb of the Hague, a strange meeting was convened. Here representatives from Israel and Germany came together for the first of many meetings at which it would be decided what sums Germany was to pay into the struggling economy of the new Israeli state. The money was reparation for lives and property lost by Jews during the Nazi regime. The financial outcome of the meetings would amount to $822 million in machinery, industrial supplies, and loans. It was of vital importance to the growth of the new country's industrial future.

A pale, taut young reporter was one of the many members of the press who covered the daily meetings of the reparations conference. As soon as each day's session was over, the slim young man rushed to his hotel room. There, on a portable Hebrew typewriter lent him by a friend in Paris, he wrote his report for the Tel Aviv daily that employed him.

The sessions were torture for Elie. He listened to the representatives from both countries bargaining over the amounts of money Germany would pay for lost lives, and inwardly shuddered at the thought that "blood money" could redeem, even partially, the enormous guilt of the

German nation. Outwardly, Elie preserved a professional appearance. No one would have guessed what these meetings meant to him, or what memories they conjured up. Perhaps there was no one in the room with a more personal involvement than he.

Only once did Elie's journalistic objectivity break down. When the conference finally adjourned, the head of the German commission walked over to the press section to thank the reporters for the coverage they had given the negotiations. It was, after all, a most delicate matter. The negotiator shook hands with all the journalists. Except for the young man from the Israeli paper *Yediot Aharonot,* who stared past his hand and walked away. He refused to shake hands with a German.

Conscientious in his working habits, and eager to please his Tel Aviv editor, Elie followed up any requests his paper made upon him, to the best of his ability. One day, he was assigned to do an interview with Pierre Mendes-France, the Jewish Premier of France. Elie was not an aggressive reporter, and he found this an impossible task: the Premier did not give interviews.

Almost in desperation, Elie thought up a plan that would enable him to get an interview with Mendes-France through the intervention of a third person, the well-known Catholic writer François Mauriac. Mauriac was known to be close to Mendes-France, and Elie reasoned that if he played his cards right, the prize-winning author might lead him right to the Premier.

Elie managed to meet the famous writer at a reception, but things did not turn out as planned. He became so interested in Mauriac that he dropped the idea of interviewing Mendes-France and arranged, instead, to meet with the author for a possible story.

Mauriac accepted Elie as an Israeli. He knew nothing

of the young man's background, so he tried to make him comfortable and spoke to him of his admiration for the Jewish people. Elie felt very much like an impostor. He had obtained this interview rather deviously and now he was poorly prepared and extremely nervous. What was more, nothing went right that morning: neither Elie's questions nor the subject Mauriac seemed intent on discussing—the life of Jesus, whom he saw as a Jew who had sacrificed himself to save his own people but instead had brought salvation to all mankind.

Convinced that the interview had failed miserably, Elie was extremely annoyed both with himself and with Mauriac. Suddenly he blurted out that six million Jews had been sacrificed deliberately only recently, and not even far from France, yet not a soul mentioned that. But he, Elie, knew this was so; he had been there and witnessed it.

Before he had finished uttering this blunt remark, Elie knew he had committed the most unprofessional blunder imaginable. He had never, in his whole life, been so totally tactless. He was shocked at himself. All he could do now was to end this meeting quickly.

Gathering up his notebook and his coat, Elie ran out of the writer's apartment and into the hall, hoping to disappear into the elevator, and out of Mauriac's life forever.

> At the same moment I heard the door opening behind me. With an infinitely humble gesture the old writer was touching my arm, asking me to come back.
>
> We returned to the drawing room and resumed our seats, one opposite the other. And suddenly the man I had just offended began to cry.

                              (*A Jew Today*, "An Interview
                                    Unlike Any Other")

Elie felt even more embarrassed and ashamed over his outburst. François Mauriac had been a member of the Resistance and a man of unimpeachable conduct during the German occupation of France. Now the old writer began to question him. But Elie hesitated, answering in monosyllables, offering only the barest details. Finally, he burst out that he could not talk about the things he had experienced, he had taken a vow of silence not to speak of them.

Elie had reason not to forget this meeting. It was the start of a close friendship with Mauriac, who received the Nobel Prize for literature in 1952. Moreover, it was a major turning point in Elie's life. As he soon came to see, the interview with the French writer, which he had believed ill-fated, was to have far-reaching results.

When Elie left Mauriac's apartment for the second time that morning, he was escorted into the hall by the aged writer. The old man urged Elie to reconsider his decision. He told him it was wrong for him to keep his thoughts to himself. He must speak out. He, Mauriac, begged him to do this.

Elie entered the elevator of Mauriac's building a changed person. The tight seal was being removed from his soul, though he was not yet aware of it. The vow of silence, that icy band in which he had imprisoned himself, was about to be released.

In the tenth year of his silence, Elie began writing about the journey from Sighet to Buchenwald. What he had seen, felt, and lost had never been shared with a single soul since the gates of Buchenwald had opened for him nine years previously.

During the next twelve months, in Paris, Elie wrote an 800-page manuscript which he called, "And the World Kept Silent." He wrote in Yiddish, the language of his youth. He accounted, step by step, for each event that had befallen his family from the end of 1941 when he was thirteen years old, to the day in 1945 when, as an orphan, he was liberated from Buchenwald by American troops.

The manuscript was printed in Argentina by a Yiddish press. Elie was less fortunate in France. No publisher there was interested in his work. Elie then condensed the manuscript considerably, from 800 to 160 pages, and translated it into the French language. The slim sheaf of pages bore the title *La Nuit* ("Night") and was dedicated to the memory of Elie's parents and his little sister, Tzipora.

Finally, Elie brought the manuscript to François Mauriac, who had encouraged him to break his vow of silence and put into words the thoughts that weighed down his soul. The famous French writer took the book of the unknown young man to his own publisher and asked him to bring it out.

17

On the speaker's rostrum of the General Assembly, the chairman gaveled the United Nations delegates to order.

"We will now have roll call. You may voice your vote in one of three ways: for, against, or abstain."

In the glassed-in press booth overlooking the huge chamber, Elie wore headphones while listening to the French version of the five-language simulcast of the proceedings. He hoped for material which he could use in the daily telegram to his Tel Aviv editor.

Elie had arrived in New York in 1956, on assignment from *Yediot Aharonot* to cover the United Nations for its Israeli readers.

Every morning he walked through the heavy doors of the tall apartment house on Riverside Drive where he had a room, newly surprised at the energy and drive he found in the American city. The refreshing view of the Hudson, the breeze-rustled leaves of the trees lining the Drive, the frantic running of passengers to catch the #5 bus: mornings in Manhattan. Elie appreciated the optimism and the cosmopolitan spirit of his new residence.

Daily he commuted to the six-block area between 42nd and 48th Streets on New York's East Side where the steel-and-green-glass complex of the United Nations Building glittered in the morning sun. The fresh clean lines of its architecture promised harmony and world

133

peace. Inside, Elie covered meetings of the General
Assembly or attended crisis-laden special sessions of the
Security Council. The workings of the United Nations
were important to Israelis. What happened in New York
and Washington was of great interest to the people of Tel
Aviv and Jerusalem, for the political events in America
might easily influence the lives of Israelis in days and
years to come. Elie preferred human-interest material to
political news. He was not too knowledgeable politically;
like many of his colleagues of the press, Elie sometimes
used political analyses from the *New York Times* as the
meat of the report he cabled to Tel Aviv in Hebrew.

To the other correspondents of the UN press corps, the
young Jew with the unruly wisps of hair sliding across his
forehead seemed remote, asocial. Because he repre-
sented an Israeli paper, they assumed him to be an
Israeli. Although he was in their midst daily, checking,
like them, for "scoops" on important events, few of the
reporters knew him. He was younger than most of them,
and always in a hurry.

Elie's colleagues were not aware that one reason for his
rapid departures from the UN premises was that he held a
second job which also required his daily attendance. The
Jewish Daily Forward, a Yiddish newspaper, had engaged
him to write articles. The four hours of writing Elie put in
at the Forward Building in Lower Manhattan every day
resulted in critical reports and current-events information aimed at the large number of American Jews who
preferred to read their news in Yiddish.

Often Elie walked home after work. After a frugal
dinner in a kosher restaurant downtown, a long walk
appealed to him, especially after the many hours behind a
desk. It was an odd sensation to move past so many people
on the New York sidewalks and to know no one. Often he
felt that he was still in France, that his life existed only in
the words which would soon be bound within the pages of

a book. He liked to think of his book, sitting on the shelves of French bookstores, waiting for a few readers to pick it up. Would anyone be moved by his words?

Elie's friend Georges Borchardt had been contacting all the American publishing houses he knew, trying to place Elie's manuscript, now translated into English. As the agent representing the French publisher of *La Nuit*, Borchardt had faith that Elie's book would find a public, but it was hard to convince American publishers that the Holocaust was a subject suitable for their readers.

Elie stood in the lobby of his apartment house, taking the mail out of his box, shaking his head over another letter of rejection he had received. "Beautifully written, but the story is too sad to appeal to our readers. We are herewith returning your manuscript." He was already familiar with the general format of those rejection slips. Every major publisher in New York had so far turned down his book. He dared not believe that this was a true mirror of the American public. Could it really mean that six million had died and now the other half of the world did not even want to know about it?

Elie turned toward the elevator. At least the postman knew who he was. After bringing so many rejection letters to 310 Riverside Drive, he had to be acquainted with the name of Elie Wiesel by this time.

Discouraging as the rejections were in the United States, they could not stop Elie from writing. Before *La Nuit* was even in print in France, he was already deeply involved with the writing of his second book. Now that he had found his "voice," writing was a necessity. Freed from his vow of silence, putting words on paper became his method of self-healing. He had learned to be an early riser as a yeshiva boy. Now he sat in front of his typewriter from six to ten o'clock every morning, paying for his ticket of readmission to life. Guilt for having survived still gnawed at him. He wrote because he had to: he was a witness, and his testimony was his reason for living.

Covering the Israeli War of Independence as a journalist furnished Elie with background material for his next book, a novel entitled *Dawn*. It is the story of a young concentration-camp survivor, Elisha, who has been assigned to kill a British officer in reprisal for the scheduled execution at dawn of a young Jewish terrorist sentenced by the British occupation forces. For Elisha, the choice is painful. He has been brought up to believe that killing is a mortal sin. Now he must kill as an act of patriotism. During the night just before the dawn when he must commit the grisly deed, Elisha sees in a vision all the people who have influenced his upbringing. His father, his mother, the Master who taught him Kabbala, appear and rebuke the young man for the act he is about to perform. Elisha feels no hatred for the "enemy," the unlucky Englishman who is the target of his assignment. Burdened by great sorrow over the murder he is due to commit, Elisha knows that a part of himself will die along with his victim.

It was Elie's first summer in New York. On an unbearably hot Sunday afternoon, he crossed Times Square, hoping to escape the baking sun in an air-conditioned movie. Before he could reach the safety of the opposite sidewalk, Elie was hit by an oncoming taxicab. He was badly injured. In the haze and pain, as his stretcher was lowered into the back of the emergency vehicle, Elie thought he heard the ambulance driver mutter, "This one will never make it," then the siren drowned out every other sound. At the hospital, too, the doctor shook his head. For days, Elie's life hung in the balance. During the many weeks of hospitalization which followed, Elie, immobilized by a body cast, his crushed bones causing him excruciating pain, reflected on the accident. Was it really a coincidence or had he perhaps walked into the path of that taxi with a subconscious death wish?

After his discharge from the hospital, during the many months while he was recuperating, Elie was housebound. He had to use a wheelchair, which made daily travel to the United Nations and to the *Jewish Daily Forward* impossible. His recent experience gave him the impetus for another novel. During the next few months, he worked on the *Le Jour*, later translated as *The Accident*.

The Accident tells the story of a death-camp survivor who has lost the will to live and wants to die so he can join his loved ones in death. Injured in an accident, he fights the efforts of his surgeon to save him. Even the love of the woman who wants to marry him is not enough to restore his desire for life. For him, the ghosts of the past are more real than what is happening in the present. Along with his family, the victim (who has no name) has also lost his faith in God, whom he blames for having forsaken him.

Describing those who, like him, are survivors of death camps and therefore beings set apart, he says:

> They eat, laugh, love—like the others. But it isn't true. They are playing, sometimes without knowing it. Anyone who has seen what they have seen cannot be like the others, cannot laugh, love, pray, bargain, suffer, have fun, or forget. Like the others.
>
> *(The Accident)*

The surgeon tries to revive the accident victim's interest in life by telling him how he saved a twelve-year-old boy given up by three other doctors. The victim is momentarily interested. What a God-like feeling it must be to save a life! But his interest does not last.

Finally, a friend lights the saving spark. Gyula, a painter, comes to the hospital to do the patient's portrait. When his young friend stubbornly persists in his effort to die, Gyula becomes angry and tries to shame him for giving up the fight. Gradually, the patient realizes that even when faith in God is dead, the friendship of one person for another may be sufficient reason to live. Sustained by the friendship of Gyula and the love of his girlfriend, Kathleen, the accident victim senses a need and a reason for returning to life.

In 1958, *La Nuit* appeared in France. It was not the first book on the Holocaust to reach the French public. It was not even the first book written by a very young person on the subject; other children and other youths had also transmitted their experiences. But *La Nuit* was altogether different, as was immediately apparent to anyone who read it. It did not dwell on physical details and horror alone. It was primarily the story of one family's fate, the relationship between a son and his father, and the impact of a devastating historical event upon the soul of a young person.

As if to prove that words fail when dealing with the subject of the Holocaust, the language of *La Nuit* is simple, in contrast to the overwhelming story it tells. This contrast is the secret of the book's power.

François Mauriac, the French Catholic who had "freed" Elie to write, and himself a writer on religious themes, penned a foreword to *La Nuit* in which he expressed his concern about the spiritual impact of the Holocaust upon its victims:

> It is, however, another aspect of this extraordinary book which has engaged me most deeply. The child who tells us his story here was one of God's elect. From the time when his conscience first

awoke, he had lived only for God and had been
reared on the Talmud, aspiring to initiation into
the cabbala, dedicated to the Eternal. Have we
ever thought about the consequence of a horror
that, though less apparent, less striking than the
other outrages, is yet the worst of all to those of us
who have faith: the death of God in the soul of a
child who suddenly discovers absolute evil?

One morning Elie's mail brought a large envelope from
Paris: a stack of clippings, gathered by his publisher, all of
them praising *La Nuit*. The book was not only a critical
success, it was selling extremely well. Bookstores were
already reordering. The happiest news came from
Georges Borchardt, who enclosed this note: "Thought
you'd want to know that you will soon be published in
America. Mr. Arthur Wang, of Hill & Wang, has read
English translation and found your book moving and
eloquent. Please see him for arrangements regarding
Night."

From his upper-floor window, Elie looked down at
Riverside Drive. He saw young mothers wheeling their
baby carriages toward the park benches, dog owners
exercising their pets along the sidewalk, old men reading
their morning newspapers in the sun. His eyes moistened
as he thought how proud his family would have been if
they could have shared his first success with him. Poor
mother, she would have enjoyed knowing that her Elie
had written a book, and that it was appearing on both
sides of the Atlantic. And Dodye too . . . Elie closed his
eyes tight, as if in great pain. Their story was the reason
for his book. He would never have had to write it if they
had not been taken from him . . .

In Elie's eyes, becoming an American citizen was an act of
fate. Coming to New York as a journalist covering the

United Nations, he had traveled on French identity papers. The accident that almost cost his life had occurred while he was visiting the United States on a year's visa. His recovery took up the greater part of that year. When Elie found out that his visa was about to expire, he was still confined to a wheelchair.

Getting around in New York in a wheelchair was not easy. Elie traveled to the foot of Manhattan in a taxi to see the U.S. Immigration Service and ask for an extension of his stay. There he was told that it was up to the French government to renew his papers for another year. Elie, wheelchair collapsed and stowed in the trunk of another taxi, visited the French Consulate in New York, only to be told that the consul could not help him. In order for his papers to be extended, Elie would have to return to Paris and see the issuing official there. He looked at the French consul in amazement. How could he go back to France in his present condition? The man shrugged his shoulders, there was nothing he could do. Not even Elie's present handicap helped in this battle with governmental bureaucracy. He remembered his early days in Paris, the shunting from one agency to another, the rubber stamps, the official indifference.

Elie made the trip between the French Consulate and the U.S. Immigration Service a number of times, each time unsuccessfully. Finally, the officer in charge at the Immigration Service said one day: "There is a way of solving the problem. Why don't you become an American citizen?"

It was the first time someone had offered him a home.

Actually, it was not that simple. Elie often wondered whether he had done the right thing by filing first papers, the preliminary step to American citizenship. Perhaps he should have gone to live in Israel. He remembered his childhood dreams of the Holy Land, the longing he had always felt for that soil, the promises the young inmates of Buchenwald made to each other to spend the rest of their lives in Israel once they were liberated.

Elie knew that many Israelis would view his decision with bitterness, would feel he had deserted them, would accuse him of seeking more success and fame than was possible in Israel. Perhaps they were right.

Since he lived in the United States, Elie was aware that he could do more here, touch more people. If his mission was to act as a witness to the recent past of the Jewish people, his testimony was not needed in Israel. If he was meant to rouse the conscience of non-Jews, his most fertile field would be in the Diaspora, the world outside of Israel. He liked to think that even those who blamed him for this choice might one day forgive him, once they saw that his contribution to Israel could be greater from the outside.

When he discovered that the accident had left his leg bones and muscles permanently weak, Elie bought a second-hand car and learned to drive. He missed the long walks home from the office, the meanderings through unfamiliar neighborhoods, the solitary strolls at night. He certainly did not like hunting for parking spaces along the crowded Upper West Side streets. But he found that owning a convertible was just what a young man his age needed when exploring new areas of the city or leaving New York behind for weekend drives through the countryside.

He resumed his daily trips to United Nations headquarters. Now he had company along the way. A childhood companion from Sighet, Mordecai Shualy, had come to New York and was also working on an assignment as a UN reporter. Every morning, Elie stopped by for his friend on West End Avenue before starting the crosstown ride to the FDR Drive. Once they had played chess together as children in their hometown, now they shared another pleasure reminding them of those long-ago days. Speeding on the expressway along the East River in an open car, the two young newspaper men celebrated their reunion by singing Hasidic songs at the top of their voices.

18

In 1960 ELIE covered the trial of Adolf Eichmann in Jerusalem for his Israeli newspaper. He sat in the courtroom day after day, staring at the Nazi killer. He tried to understand what had made this man so particularly evil. He sought to find something extraordinary in Eichmann's manner and personality. Instead, he saw a drab, bland individual who used dates and statistics to defend his life. Elie wasn't satisfied. He had expected so monumental a killer to look and act in a grotesque manner. How could anyone so ordinary, both in looks and behavior, be the henchman of murderers like Himmler and Heydrich? He could not comprehend that the man in charge of transport for the systematic "final solution" was the same dull, vapid person now standing before the judges and reciting the facts and figures of his heinous crimes with the calm demeanor of an engineer giving a company report.

Two years later Elie returned to Germany for a visit. Seventeen years earlier, when he had walked out of the gates of Buchenwald, Elie would not have believed that one day he would return to the country which had deprived him of everything he had once held precious. For years his heart was heavy with hate: for the country, for its people, even for its language. Elie believed the hatred would be his for his lifetime. Then he decided to test himself and the country which had so grieved him, to

143

understand what after-effect the Holocaust had had on them both.

The trip was his own decision, not an assignment, but two professional engagements were planned for his stay in Germany: a radio appearance and an evening of readings from *Night*. Between these, Elie had time to observe. From conversations with other young writers he learned that the Germany of the 1960's was in no way what he had expected. He was surprised at the general complacency. Not only was Germany doing better financially and industrially, everything within the country was at its peak: production, international trade, the arts. Elie met no one who wanted to be reminded of other days, other times. No one spoke of guilt or remorse. After his Munich lecture, a young German writer came to the stage to meet him and said: "I heard you read tonight, but I must confess that concentration-camp literature leaves me cold. I just don't understand it."

After forty-eight hours, Elie left Germany. He had learned two things of importance to him. He had learned that Germany, seventeen years later, felt neither fear nor shame for what had happened. The memory of the Holocaust lingered with the victims, not with the nation which had inflicted it. The second thing Elie realized was that he no longer hated.

The strong feelings that had troubled him for so many years no longer existed. His hate had evaporated, just as Germany's memory had. In Germany, Elie found, there was nothing left to hate. Elie felt as if he had betrayed the dead. Somehow, by hating the killers, it had been possible to vindicate the victims. Now there was nothing. Except sadness.

In the "pilgrimage to the past" which had occupied Elie's mind during his early years in New York, one constant theme predominated: relationships. Elie pondered the relationship between God and man, and that between man and man. Out of his ponderings came two novels, *The Town Beyond the Wall* and *The Gates of the Forest*.

In *The Town Beyond the Wall*, Michael, the hero, returns to his hometown. He is trying to find and understand the Others, those people who, through apathy, aided the destructive work of the enemy. During the years of his wanderings, it is not the Nazis he has remembered, but the "face in the window," the spectator. Michael has never been able to fathom how anyone could stand by and watch, without feeling guilty, as a large part of the town's population was rounded up for deportation.

At the same time, Michael needs to free himself of the God whom he is trying to deny for having forsaken him. But the very act of defiance only convinces him that God does exist. For how could Michael deny Him unless He existed?

Michael has a friend, Pedro, who supports and guides him, much as Gyula, the artist, helped the patient in *The Accident*. Pedro remains on the outside, on safe territory, while Michael arrives in his old hometown, now under Communist rule.

The same spectator who was witness and complacent bystander at the deportation of the town's Jews is now confronted by Michael. He becomes an informer, reporting Michael to the Communist police, and they imprison him.

In prison, Michael saves the life of a retarded and mute young boy when another prisoner tries to kill him. In his desperate attempt to awaken the boy to life, Michael finds his own salvation. He is helping another human being, thereby protesting against inhumanity. He is fighting for someone else's life. In the process Michael learns to value his own existence and to realize its purpose.

In *The Town Beyond the Wall,* Elie describes Michael's return to his old hometown almost as if he were recalling his own memories of such a return. His words evoked the town as if he had actually visited it, yet it was Elie's imagination that painted the picture.

Michael wanted "to see what's become of the city while I was away. A little as though a dead man were able to come back to earth after his funeral. To see his friends, and his enemies, who go on living, fighting, cheating as though he'd never existed."

In the autumn of 1964, Elie returned to Sighet for his own half-dreaded, half-wished-for reunion with the town of his childhood.

"It sometimes seems to me that ever since I left it, I have been spending all my time telling about this town which gave me everything and then took it all away."

It was twenty years since the Sunday in spring when everyone he knew had walked to the railroad station in Sighet, never to return. Now he had come back alone. What did he expect to find?

In the many dreams Elie had dreamed during his wanderings, the town always appeared to him just as he had left it. In his mind he walked through its streets and saw the Hasidim in their long dark coats, hurrying to their sanctuaries. He stopped near the market and smelled the aroma of fresh produce, nodded to the merchants, then searched out his teachers for a chat to clear up a point of talmudic reference. In his fantasies, he approached his house, walked into the garden, up the back porch into the kitchen, where his mother was preparing a Sabbath meal. It would all be there on his return to Sighet. He would find it and "I shall feel guilty for having dreamed that they were dead."

But there was another aspect to his dreams. There were nightmares of fear when "I would be the only one to return, I would walk through the streets, aimlessly, without seeing a familiar face, an open look. And I would go mad with loneliness."

In the fall of the year 1964, Elie came back, at night, in a taxi which drove him over the mountains and into the heart of Sighet. Everything was the way he remembered it, the buildings, the town square, the Street of the Jews. He arrived at midnight when the town was asleep. He stood on the sidewalk and stared at the empty town square. He recalled the last time he had seen it: filled with hundreds of people, burdened with bundles and suitcases, as they wound their way around the square while a hot sun shone over the town.

Elie checked into the local hotel. He remembered it as the height of luxury and good living. Now that he was a grown man who had sufficient funds to rent a room there, the hotel had become, like the town, a reflection of life under socialism, "without pomp, without comfort." He found that, "like everything else, it had lied to the child I had been."

He roamed the streets that night, then headed for the most important spot he had come to see: the house of his childhood. Everything he remembered led back here. He stood at the gate leading into the garden and took a mental photograph. He listened to the vibrations of the trees in the wind, smelled the scents of the garden. The picture would have to last. He would not come back again.

The bark of a dog stopped Elie from entering the garden—as if he were a burglar. The pain and rage were unbearable. He fled the scene and spent the rest of the night on a bench in the town square, unable to sleep, tormented by thoughts and memories.

The next morning, he mingled with the people in the town. He looked for familiar faces and found none. No one paid him the slightest attention. It was as if he had never existed here. When he walked past his former home again, he saw the new owner come out of it. But there was no reason to speak to him. It was too late.

No one recognized him. His grade-school teacher, whom Elie met again, did not recall that he had been in his class. A former neighbor, once very friendly with Elie's family, did not remember him. Only in one place was Elie certain that this was truly Sighet, the town of his birth: in the cemetery. While he stood there, burning candles to the memory of those who belonged here but had died elsewhere, an old man with a prayerbook appeared beside him. Together Elie and the old man said the El Mole Rachamim, the chant recited at Jewish funerals. They tried to give peace to the missing dead who should have found their last rest here.

Twenty-four hours after he had come, Elie left Sighet. Did he regret coming back? Whatever he sought, he had not found there. Neither in the shadows of the night nor in the noise of the town's daily life had he found the past he remembered. Finally, he had to admit, "my journey to the source of all events had been merely a journey to nothingness."

Like a musician composing variations on a theme, Elie—preoccupied with the idea of going home to a place which no longer exists—wrote a number of versions of his trip to Sighet in story form. One such story, "The Watch," appears in a later book, *One Generation After*. It pictures the emotions of a man returning to his hometown after twenty years. He visits his parents' house—now occupied by strangers—and realizes that he is no longer remembered in the town which has been on his mind during all the years he was absent from it. He searches for—and finds—the Bar Mitzvah watch which he, as a young boy, had hidden in the ground on the day of the Jewish exodus.

Somehow it is the watch, his first and last gift from his parents, which is the most meaningful symbol of the life he and his family once led here. It is all that remains.

The visitor contemplates his treasure, delighted to find the watch in the spot he remembered. It is covered with dirt and rust, but he will have it restored to usefulness and beauty. Carrying the watch in his hand, he leaves the garden. Suddenly he stops.

Slowly, he steps back into his parents' garden. Carefully, he reburies the watch in the same spot where it has lain for the last twenty years. He has decided that he no longer wants it. It will remain in the ground where he once left it for safekeeping against the day when he and his family would return to claim it.

The watch will stay in its hiding place, but someday, he hopes, a child living in Sighet will come upon this spot and will find it. Perhaps that child will ask his parents why this once-beautiful watch came to be buried in their garden. Perhaps they will tell him of the people who lived here and were dispersed from the town because they were Jews. And then the watch, so loved and treasured by its first owner, who was forced to give it up, will have served its true purpose. It will truly be a reminder of time. Of a time which has vanished. Along with a whole people.

19

In the hasidic tradition a *m'shulach* is a mysterious messenger of fate to whom nothing is impossible. It is just such a role that Elie gave to the hero of *The Gates of the Forest*.

Gavriel is a messenger, a spirit who moves from the past to the present. Like Elie, he is "the last survivor." And like most Wiesel heroes, his name contains the letters *El*, the Hebrew word for God. Elie uses special care in choosing names, for they reflect his view of the characters he invents. Each one carries a "mystical part," the strongly spiritual fragment which comes from God. So his heroes act out what Elie calls "the power in naming."

The title of the book refers to the symbolism of studying the Kabbala: "There are a thousand and one gates to the orchard of mystic truth. Each person must look for and find his own. The gate that opens on the past and the gate that opens on the future are one and the same."

Four separate sections make up *The Gates of the Forest*: Gavriel moves in and out of them all. He first appears to Gregor, the survivor, in the forest, informing him that his father and all the members of the ghetto have been killed. From the forest Gregor finds his way to the home of Maria, a former family servant. She hides him, pretending he is her mute nephew, and Gregor soon gains the confidence of all the important people in her village.

150

When Gregor takes part in the local school play—the Judas story—the villagers reenact the age-old hostility and Gregor becomes their target. Gregor reveals that he is a Jew, not a deaf-mute, and appeals to the conscience of the villagers. He is saved from their anger by escaping back to the forest, where he joins a band of Jewish partisans, headed by a former friend and protector, Leib.

One of the partisans, Yehuda, is killed in the forest. His comrades bury him and say Kaddish over him. Gregor leaves the forest in a plot to rescue Gavriel from prison in a nearby town. Involved in helping him are Leib and his girlfriend, Clara. Leib is arrested and killed. Clara and Gregor remain behind: lovers tied together by a common guilt, their relationship with Leib.

Living in the forest is easy, Wiesel seems to be saying. It is a harder task to face the world with its many demands and directions. In the book's last scene, Gregor is in a Brooklyn prayer hall, among pious Hasidim, and there he comes to realize an important truth: God may not need man, but man cannot do without God. While in the synagogue of the Hasidim, Gregor says Kaddish over the dead of his past. He returns to faith. Then he returns to his wife, Clara, to help her regain the road back to life.

In writing *The Gates of the Forest*, Elie Wiesel took a further step toward the world of the living. The book no longer echoes the deep despair of his earlier writings. He is now able to give up the dead to the peace they deserve. He has released them. Now he is himself able to take up life and love.

"My name is Lily Edelman."

The short, motherly woman who shook Elie's hand at a public gathering had extraordinary eyes, lively and penetrating. They sparkled with pleasure at meeting him.

"My husband and I have read your last two books. Young man, you are a remarkable writer."

In his shy, European way, Elie bowed at the compliment. He did not know that Lily Edelman was no cocktail-party flatterer.

"I'd like you to meet my husband. Nathan teaches."

Her face beamed under its coif of braided dark brown hair, flecked with gray. Her husband appeared out of a milling crowd and she introduced the two men.

Dr. Nathan Edelman did not only teach, as his wife modestly put it, he was chairman of the Romance Languages department at Johns Hopkins University. Lily Edelman, who told Elie that she reviewed Jewish books for a national magazine, also did not mention that she was director of Adult Jewish Education for B'nai B'rith, and the head of that organization's Lecture Bureau. Later, Elie found out that she was a gifted, versatile writer herself and had already produced several books and texts.

He liked her at once. Beneath her dignified manner, he sensed a razor-sharp intelligence and a keen desire to help others.

"Why don't you send me a copy of your new book to review?" Lily Edelman asked him that day. "Better yet, if you need a translator for the next one, I'd like to apply for the job."

After the publication of *The Town Beyond the Wall* in 1964, Elie received the first of the many prizes and literary awards which were to continue coming his way from then on. In France, he was given the Prix Rivarol, in the United States, the National Jewish Book Council Award. The prizes helped to push the name of Elie Wiesel into prominence as a new writer in the United States after his books were already read in France and in Israel.

Elie's connection with Lily Edelman resulted not only in a close friendship, and her translation of several of his books, but also in her championing him as a new talent to many of her associates. In 1966, Elie became the recipient of B'nai B'rith's first annual Jewish Heritage Award for Excellence in Literature, which made him even better known.

The young man with the melancholy eyes and the soft French accent quickly became a charismatic attraction on the lecture circuit. Elie on the platform was a tragic, haunting, mysterious figure. He brought to his audiences fragments of his experiences in the recent past; he used every occasion to stir the conscience of his listeners.

Elie used these lectures as a means of speaking out on current Jewish and world concerns. Gently he chided his listeners for their apathy, past and present. He reminded them that the future of Judaism and the world lay in their hands. Now he was able to reach thousands of people through his personal appearances. To them he was a link with a vanished world, he was a witness.

> Whoever lives through a trial or takes part in an event that weighs on man's destiny or frees him, is dutybound to transmit what he has seen, felt and feared. The Jew has always been obsessed by the obligation. He has always known that to live an experience or create a vision, and not transform it into link and promise, is to turn it into a gift to death.
>
> *(One Generation After)*

When he stands on a lecture podium, before the crowds who fill all available seats on the night of a Wiesel talk, Elie remembers the maggidim of his hometown. He has never forgotten how, as a youngster, he ran to hear every one of the Saturday-afternoon speakers. Like the story-teller-preachers of his childhood, Elie uses Hasidic stories and legends to transmit his message. Only now he is the maggid whom the people come to hear.

20

"I WENT TO RUSSIA drawn by the silence of its Jews. I brought back their cry," Elie said in the introduction to *The Jews of Silence*, a compilation of several articles he wrote for his newspaper after his visit to the Soviet Union during the Holy Days of 1965.

It was Elie's personal wish to go to Russia. Like everyone else, he had heard the rumors that the Soviet Jews were being persecuted. He wanted to see for himself whether these rumors were true. He wanted to see the Jews who had survived the German slaughter of Jews in Russia and were now living under Communist dictatorship. Why were they suffering, and what was the nature of their pain? Did they really want to remain Jews and transmit their Jewishness to their children? If so, what prevented them from doing so?

Elie had been in Moscow only a few hours when a stranger approached him. "Do you know what is happening to us?" he asked in Yiddish. He disappeared into the crowd, an anonymous figure and face. Elie could not say whether he was young or old, student or businessman. Similar episodes occurred in other cities Elie visited. A man touched his arm in a crowd, another winked at him in recognition; sometimes he found notes thrust into his pockets. It became clear soon enough: each person who contacted him wanted Elie to know he was recognized as a Jew, but the stranger was afraid to reveal himself. Why

154

was there such a climate of fear? What did these people have to dread?

Elie felt as if he had been transported backward in time. He was no longer in Russia but in the Spain of Isabella and Ferdinand—the age of the Marranos, Spanish Jews who had been converted to Catholicism but continued to practice Judaism in secret, even though they were in constant peril of death at the stake should their secret be discovered.

The suspicion and fear he found in Russia puzzled Elie. He looked for ordinary people to talk to, not official spokespersons; he wanted to get at the truth of life in the Soviet Union. But the people he met seemed terrorized captives on the brink of some awful abyss. Did they fear imprisonment for speaking with a foreigner, he wondered, or was it communicating with Jews which was forbidden?

Whenever anyone was brave enough to speak, the message was always the same: "Tell it all! Do not forget us!" But what was there to tell? Enclosed in their own web of silent fear, Soviet Jews left it to Elie to discover what they had no words to describe. Soon he learned that they were worried about informers lurking in their midst. Jews themselves, these informers mingled in crowds, attended synagogue services, and reported to the government all they had seen and heard. Afraid of the informers, the Jews of Soviet Russia wrapped themselves into a cocoon of silence.

While attending Sukkot services at the synagogue in Kiev, Elie finally received a "full report" on the state of Soviet Jewry. During the service he heard some bits and snatches of Hebrew which did not belong to the prayer being recited at that moment. Listening carefully, Elie was able to pick out phrases and sentences interspersed with the prayers. His informant—apparently an old man sitting behind him who to all intents and purposes was deeply absorbed in his prayers—told him that Jewish life in Kiev was very difficult, that the teaching of Torah was outlawed, that anti-Semitism was widespread, and worst of all, that the Jewish spirit was deteriorating. Elie never had occasion to speak with his informant, but the things he learned confirmed his suspicions, and he was grateful for the courage and ingenuity of the old man, who had managed to tell his sad story despite the tight rein of the synagogue leaders.

It was heartening to return to Moscow and worship there on Simchat Torah, the Rejoicing in the Law. The experience awaiting Elie in Moscow was one he would never forget. As a guest he walked in the procession of dignitaries who carried the holy scrolls around the old main synagogue. He prayed with the elders within the sanctuary, but it was on the outside that the surprise awaited him. Close to 30,000 youths had gathered there, the young people of Moscow, from all social strata, singing Jewish songs and dancing in celebration of the age-old commandment to honor the Law. Elie saw youngsters throwing their comrades up in the air and catching them in a sea of outstretched hands. The joy of celebration was infectious. Having been told that Soviet Jewish youth wanted no part of Judaism, Elie was brought to the point of tears at hearing these young Jews sing "Am Yisroel Hai—the Jewish People Lives."

If Elie brought out any message from Russia, it was the plea of the people to whom he had spoken: "Cry out, cry out until you have no more strength to cry. You must enlist public opinion, you must turn to those with influence, you must involve the governments—the hour is late."

The Jews of Silence, published in 1966, was that cry. It

pulled aside the veil and drew attention to people who until then had been hidden in the shadows. It stimulated interest. Soviet Jewry soon became the focus of many specially formed groups and committees, and in the early 1970's Jewish emigration from Russia to Israel and the United States began to accelerate.

Elie's visit to Russia in 1965 included an experience that haunted him for some time afterward. While praying at a Kol Nidre service, he was attracted by the congregation's old rabbi. The man's obvious resignation and hopelessness made so striking a picture of defeat that all through the service Elie found himself waiting for something to happen.

His artistic imagination caused him to visualize the drama which might unfold if the rabbi were suddenly to throw caution away and reveal the anguish he felt. Suppose it would all explode into rage, that fear and isolation which imprisoned the rabbi and his congregation? How would they show their real feelings to the world? In the weeks after his departure from Russia, thoughts about the old rabbi and his unspoken feelings remained with Elie. The intensity of the experience grew. Perhaps it was up to him to express what the tired, defeated rabbi no longer had the strength to reveal. "That was when the idea occurred to me to offer him another chance to redeem himself and become the accuser."

Elie's play, *Zalmen; or, The Madness of God*, was the chance he sought for the unforgettable old rabbi to become a spokesman for the oppressed, drained victims of a godless, totalitarian society.

In the play, Zalmen, the synagogue beadle, pushes the rabbi to declare himself. Since he is already considered a madman, divorced from reality, Zalmen can act and speak freely. He is, therefore, the ideal tool to drive the rabbi into action: prompting the sermon in which the old man breaks his silence and reveals his fears.

In 1966 Elie Wiesel returned to the Soviet Union for a second visit. On Simchat Torah, again standing on Arkhipova Street in Moscow, he convinced himself that the spectacle he had witnessed here the previous year had not been a figment of his imagination. The street leading up to Moscow's main synagogue was thronged by thousands of Jewish students. singing and dancing in celebration. For hours the area vibrated to the songs and movements of the youngsters, who had come here to express solidarity with their people, with the State of Israel, and with their history.

Suddenly, without warning, the lights went off. The whole block was dark. Someone in authority had ordered the festivities to end; turning out the lights was an official signal for everyone to go home. For a few moments there was stunned silence, until the crowd realized that the darkness was not a mistake, and the lights would not be turned on again this night.

Soon there was a roar of protest in the dark. Moments later, one youngster lit a rolled-up newspaper to make a torch. He was followed in this by his nearest neighbors. Within moments the scene was illuminated by the burning paper torches of thousands of people, lighting up the street and proving that no one had left to go home.

> I don't remember how long it lasted. I only remember the dreamlike quality of the scene: students climbing onto a balcony, torches in hand, chanting in Hebrew and Russian: "Am Israel Hai, the Jewish people lives and will go on living!" And

the crowd answering thunderously: "Hurrah, hur-
raaah!"

"Well?" asked a man I had met on a previous
visit.

"What do you think now? Are you more
confident than last year?"

(*One Generation After,*
"Russian Sketches")

In a 1979 interview, Elie was asked his response to the
Soviet Jewry movement which had been initiated by the
publication of *The Jews of Silence* and *Zalmen*. He
replied: "It was a miracle. If anyone had told me that one
day we'd see the Russian Jews emigrating in such numbers, I would have thought they were crazy. Nobody
would believe it could happen in my time."

21

MANY READERS, familiar with the writings of Elie Wiesel, saw his quest to awaken the world to the plight of Soviet Jewry as a direct result of the bitter lessons learned during the Holocaust. Millions of lives might have been saved, he implied, had the writers, the politicians, and the leaders of important Western nations spoken out forcefully while it mattered.

"A Plea for the Dead," an essay its author called "a protest against history," was written and published in 1968. In it, Elie insisted that finding causes or reasons for the Holocaust was all too often a hindsight game played by historians and scientists.

> And in this game—it is really nothing else—it is quite easy to blame the dead, to accuse them of cowardice or complicity. . . . Now, this game has a humiliating aspect. To insist on speaking in the name of the dead—and to say: these are their motivations, these the considerations that weakened their wills, to speak in their name—this is precisely to humiliate them. The dead have earned something other than this posthumous humiliation. I never before understood why, in the Jewish faith, anything that touches corpses is impure. Now I begin to understand.

"A Plea for the Dead" is the last of the fifteen stories and memoirs Elie included in the volume *Legends of Our Time*, published in 1968. Each story, personal and poignant, concerns people or incidents which have shaped his thinking. Each portrait, whether of his father or his teachers, holds a universe. By remembering, Elie extends the lives of those who once loved and influenced him.

In France, in the late 1960's, a friend presents Elie with a book. It is a volume of photographs and text published by the government of Poland, a pictorial history of some of the Jews of Poland during the Holocaust. Elie leafs through the book. The pictures are painful to look at. They tear him apart. He turns the pages and finds a full-length photograph of an old man surrounded by laughing German soldiers who are entertaining themselves by cutting off his white beard with their daggers. For a moment, Elie's heart stops. He recognizes the face ot the old man at once: it is Dodye Feig.

It had been Elie's fate to see his mother walk away into the fiery night of Auschwitz, holding his little sister by the hand. He had watched his father fade out of life in Buchenwald. But he had never known the exact facts surrounding his grandfather's deportation. Now he knew. Thanks to a photograph of a tormented old man taken only moments before his captors made an end of him in the forest dimly visible in the picture's background.

Elie wrote a touching story about his grandfather. It understated Elie's terrible pain at finding Dodye Feig in a photograph taken during the last hour of his life. It painted, instead, the portrait of a noble man whose nobility and strength, based on deep faith, served him well in his last moments on earth.

The memory of his grandfather has never left Elie. He,

to whom Dodye was the personification of everything a good Jew should be, set a loving monument to his grandfather.

> I owe him my love of tradition, my passion for the Jewish people and its unfortunate children. And he, who never read a novel, is a presence in my novels. My old men often bear his features, sing the way he did and, like him, disarm melancholy with the magic of words.

> (A Jew Today,
> "Portraits from the Past")

June 5, 1967. Israelis awoke to the radio announcement of Kol Israel, "Egypt this morning launched a land-and-air attack." Within seconds the news circled the globe.

In New York, Elie called the airlines for the first available flight to Tel Aviv, then packed his slim suitcase and his travel typewriter. Within hours, he was on his way to the Middle East. As a Jew and as a reporter, it was a necessity to be there when the future of the young State of Israel was endangered.

From the very birth of their state, Israelis had expected that one day the strong feelings of their neighbors, fomented by the constant agitation of the Soviet Union, would boil over against them once more. The leaders of the Arab states, especially Egypt's President Gamal Nasser, had been working full speed toward another war. The seething anger of Arab defeat in 1948 had never cooled down completely. Israel knew it was only a matter of time before she would be attacked again. Now that day had come.

As he walked down the steps of the El Al plane, headed

for the customs hall of Lod airport, Elie was amazed at the
long streams of passengers awaiting entry. Every available seat on Israel-bound flights was booked for days
ahead. Instead of exiting from the war zone, Jews,
non-Jews, reporters, and volunteers were flocking toward it, anxious to help Israel during her trauma.

Like Elie, these travelers knew how much depended
on this war. If Israel fell, the survival of Jews in other parts
of the world would also be doubtful. The Jews of the
Diaspora might not be able to endure the annihilation of
their brothers twice within one lifetime. The existence of
the State of Israel had given new pride and moral support
to Jewish people wherever they lived, even within the
confines of the Soviet Union. As Elie was to write, "The
shadow of Auschwitz finally enveloped Jerusalem."

This time things turned out differently. On June 10,
1967, it was all over: the Egyptians fled across the desert,
leaving behind their burned-out tanks; the Syrians gave
up the Golan Heights amid heavy casualties; in Jerusalem
the Jordanians retreated and Israeli paratroopers liberated the holy places—for the first time in nineteen years
the Old City was Jewish again. Israel had relied on her
own strength to defend herself. When the test came, she
was ready. It had cost the blood and lives of her sons, but
there would not be another Holocaust.

> I saw Israel at war; I can therefore testify in its
> behalf. In the Old City of Jerusalem, barely
> reconquered, I saw hardened paratroopers pray
> and weep for the first time in their lives; I saw
> them in the thick of battle, gripped by an ancient
> collective fervor, kiss the stones of the Wall and
> commune in a silence as elusive as it was pure; I
> saw them, as in a dream, jump two thousand years

into the past, renewing their bond with legend, memory and the mysterious tradition of Israel.

(One Generation After)

But what about the future? Will there be more wars, more friction and agitation in a region so constantly beset by tension and hatred?

In 1970, Elie publishes a collection of pieces entitled *One Generation After,* translated in collaboration with Lily Edelman. In the book, Elie writes an imaginary letter "To a Concerned Friend" which he finishes with these words:

> Of course, like you, I hope with all my heart that one day Jew and Arab, reconciled for the sake of their children, will live in peace, without the aspirations of the one limiting the other's. That this reflects the deepest vision of the Israelis, I firmly believe. Threatened by their own extremists, Arab leaders, unfortunately do not dare take the hand extended to them, and therein lies the tragedy.

When *One Generation After* appeared, Elie had reached a turning point. For him, this tenth book meant a time of summing up. Twenty-five years had now gone by since he had emerged from the gates of the "Kingdom of Night," the terminology he used for the extermination camp experience. He felt that this book would be the last in which the Holocaust was his central theme.

To a Paris interviewer Elie revealed that he had always known it would take him at least ten books to present his thoughts on the Holocaust. He had known it from the moment when, as a survivor, he stared at his image in a mirror after liberation and found "a corpse staring back." Although his books established Elie as the chronicler of the darkest period in the history of the Jewish people, grave doubts remain in his mind to this day as to whether his efforts had any effect. His books were prompted by "the survivor's urge to communicate what he has seen and endured," and many readers were stirred by them. But Elie himself has had people say to him: "Accounts of the Holocaust bore me."

For one whole generation, Elie had written a memorial to those lost in the Kingdom of Night. He had written their stories—in his novels, essays, stories, and news reports—because he felt the victims needed someone to record their unhappy pilgrimage on earth. But he needed the victims too. Their memory kept him alive, gave his work a purpose, and his survival a justification. And yet, he asked himself, how can it ever be explained? Who has the right to speak for the dead who are not here to defend their own views?

Elie had reached one conclusion: the Holocaust will never be explained. "It cannot be put into words. I have tried and only showed the absence of words, the impossibility of words."

For a while, Elie's had been the most compelling voice to tell the story; now others had taken it up from him. But, he realized, it would not be until his generation was gone that anyone would know how effective his voice had been. And time was running out. "The ghosts will have to accept the inevitable. Soon there will be no one left to speak of them, no one left to listen."

For Elie, *One Generation After* marks the point from which he will concern himself with other topics, seek new directions. "The teller of tales has turned the page."

On the eve of Passover 1969, Jews all over the world were preparing their households for yet another celebration of the festival of freedom.

In the Jewish quarter of Jerusalem, people hurry to get home for the Seder, old Hasidim in long coats and white stockings head for their prayer halls, Jewish merchants bar the entrances to their shops with wrought-iron gates. A gentle spring breeze from the Judean hills blows over the city. An air of holiday expectancy hovers over Jerusalem.

Inside the ancient Ramban Synagogue, named for the great Jewish philosopher and scholar of the Middle Ages, Moses Nachmanides, there is peace and a sense of continuity. Two people standing before its bima receive blessings over their union in marriage.

Elie Wiesel is marrying Marion Erster Rose. It is his first marriage, her second.

It is a very private event. Only a handful of people comprise the wedding party and listen to Professor Saul Lieberman, Elie's Talmud teacher and close friend, as he reads the marriage ceremony.

Elie had met Marion through friends in New York. A blonde with luminous dark eyes, Marion had warmth and charm. She was as confident and vivacious as Elie was serious and intense. Like him, she was born in Europe. Raised in Vienna, she, too, had been in a concentration camp. She understood his background and shared his concerns. The experiences both had lived through in their early years bonded them together now. A superb linguist, Marion would become an enormous help to her husband. Her translation of Elie's books from French into English would establish them in a partnership which depended heavily on Marion's sensitive interpretation of all the nuances of his writing.

For Elie, marriage was the most positive step he had

yet taken in his personal life. Those who knew him well rejoiced with him for finding Marion. His readers, who saw his life mirrored in his writings, hoped that Elie would find in marriage a new beginning for himself.

Why had he waited so long? Elie was the first to acknowledge that he might not have been ready for marriage during those long years he spent alone. The events of his youth had left ghosts behind. He needed to free himself of those ghosts, find his balance, before he could commit himself to such a major step as marriage and family. And, of course, he was waiting for "the right person."

For someone as aware of symbols as Elie, beginning married life during the auspicious season of spring and hope was a meaningful gesture.

There were other reasons for believing hope would be an important ingredient of the new Wiesel household. Jennifer, Marion's daughter from her previous marriage, would live with them. The presence of the pre-teenager was a daily reminder to Elie of how necessary it was to think of the future, not only of the past. He was just about Jennifer's age when his own world was destroyed. This child's world must be preserved and improved.

In the hush of the old synagogue, Marion and Elie looked at each other and recited the Shehekhiyanu, the prayer of thanksgiving: "Blessed art Thou, Lord our God, Who has protected and preserved us, and brought us to this day."

22

A *Beggar in Jerusalem,* Elie's first book to come out after his marriage, is dedicated to Marion, his wife. It was first published in France, where it was a tremendous success, selling over 100,000 copies and winning the Prix Medicis for Elie, before coming out in the United States in 1970, where it was also a best seller.

According to Jewish tradition, when the Messiah comes to bring redemption, he will be found among the beggars. The beggar, in Jewish folk literature, is a magic figure. He possesses hidden, powerful qualities: he might be a prince in disguise, the world's richest man, or a poor fool. But the beggar knows truths the rest of the world does not. He carries a message for those who try to decipher it.

Those beggars who gather at the Jerusalem Wall see and hear secrets revealed to no others. For them past and present merge: time does not matter here. They sit in "the haunted square in this city where nothing is lost and nothing dispersed." They are the keepers of Jerusalem's history; in them are mirrored the events which befall Jews throughout the world.

Into their domain enters David, a soldier in the Israeli army platoon which is sent to liberate the Wall. David is searching for his friend Katriel, who has disappeared just as the platoon reaches its objective. Katriel is not only David's best friend; he is his support, his source of strength. David himself is a death-camp survivor, heavily burdened by the past, which has robbed him of his family and home.

David sits with the beggars, who tell him of their contributions toward winning the just-completed war. While they talk, there are flashbacks into Jewish history. Predominant are the scenes from David's childhood: his family appears, his hometown and the people who once lived in it—all gone because of the Holocaust. Earlier episodes of history surface: talmudic legends and tales, events in the lives of famous teachers and rabbis. The Jewish past meshes with the Jewish present; through it the beggars at the Wall become performers-and-audience-in-one for this kaleidoscopic theater. They are the ears and mouths who hear and tell the Jewish story.

In the timeless tapestry of *A Beggar in Jerusalem*, David's tale is only one strand. The tale begins and ends in front of the Wall, which was reunited with its memories on the day in 1967 when Israeli troops liberated it. Past and present come together for David as he realizes that his friend Katriel is lost, that he will never find him again. The young soldier regrets having survived. He is surrounded only by the spirits of those he remembers. But he knows he must go on, for his survival serves a purpose: he is the only one who remembers, and he will not let others forget. If it is his mission to tell the story of what he has seen, it is theirs to listen.

Katriel is lost, but David will survive. Just so, the State of Israel was born after most of the Jewish people died without seeing their Promised Land. Judaism will live, despite all attempts to destroy it.

A full house awaited Elie in the Amphithéâtre Descartes at the Sorbonne, where he was starting a lecture series. He stood on the lecture platform, facing the rows of seats curving upward toward the back of the great auditorium. Emotion washed over him as his eyes searched for a certain section in the hall. Somewhere among those seats in the back, a penniless young refugee once attended courses in this very auditorium. Struggling with the French language, the impoverished student surely would not have believed that a day would come when he would turn teacher and lecture from this podium to an audience that paid to hear him speak on his favorite subject—the lives of the Hasidic Masters.

"God sees, God watches. He is in every life, in every thing. The world hinges on His will." Elie quoted the Besht, the Baal Shem Tov, founder of Hasidism, in French. The words fell softly from his lips. How long ago was it that he had first heard these lines as a child, in Sighet?

Thursday nights in Manhattan: Elie Wiesel's lecture series at the YMHA's Kauffman Auditorium is always sold out. The teller of tales makes time and place melt away, as he recounts stories he heard his grandfather tell, recites legends he first encountered in the House of Study of his youth.

> "Beware, your coachman is dangerous and wicked," said the Baal Shem to one of his followers. "I saw him walk by the church without crossing himself. If he does not love his God, why then would he love you?"

Listening to Elie's softly accented voice, a listener can imagine the candlelit closeness of a small room somewhere in the upper story of a Hasidic synagogue far off in the Eastern Europe of his ancestors, sensing the simple environment of the Tzaddik and his followers, where joy tried to replace sadness.

When he speaks of the Baal Shem, Elie tells his audiences that the Besht never allowed his disciples to write down anything about him. Whatever knowledge existed about him or his teachings came down by word-of-mouth from one generation of his followers to the next. In the thousands of retellings events became legends, and no one knew whether they were actual facts or truth embellished with the patina of age and repetition.

The tales told about the Besht were true in the mouths and hearts of those repeating them. They were true because their tellers believed in them with devotion and fervor. The most important message carried in these tales was that a living relationship exists between God and His people.

> He told them what they wanted to hear: that every one of them existed in God's memory, that every one of them played a part in his people's destiny, each in his own way and according to his means.

Reconstructing the Baal Shem's message to his followers was Elie's gift to his audiences.

From the notes he had prepared for his Paris and New York lectures, Elie worked out the backbone of the book he had always hoped to write. The result was *Souls on Fire*, published in 1972.

When he decided to write a full-length book on Hasidism, Elie concentrated on the profiles of some Masters he found most interesting. All during his childhood he had heard the legends pertaining to various Tzaddikim. Sometimes a legend was even credited to more than one Master. But each Master was special in his personality and in his relationships.

Elie began with the Founder, the Baal Shem Tov. Because he grew up in the Carpathian Mountains, where legends about the Baal Shem abounded, it was easy for Elie to identify with him. Thinking about the Besht enabled him to recall his own childhood. But there were also tales about other Masters. Each Master had been a charismatic leader whose kingdom offered his followers what they needed: asylum from the overwhelming storms of the outside world, a way to find happiness through a strong belief in God, love, and the eventual coming of the Messiah.

Elie's reasons for compiling *Souls on Fire* were purely personal. As he wrote in the book's final pages,

> . . . he was seduced by the idea of bringing back to life some of the characters that peopled his universe, the universe of his childhood. They fascinate and haunt him still, ever more. For the Hasidic movement that preached brotherhood and reconciliation became the altar upon which an entire people was immolated. Sometimes the child in me tells me that the world did not deserve this Law, this love, this spirit and this song that accompany man on his lonely road. The world did not deserve the fables the Hasidim told them; that is why they were the first to be caught and swept away in the turmoil.

In describing the eight Masters, and their disciples, who are the "souls on fire," Elie carefully points out that none of them was afraid to speak back to God. In fact, he shows that quarreling with God is part of the Jewish tradition. "To challenge God is permissible, even required," he states. "One can say anything as long as it is for man, not against him."

Reviewers writing about *Souls on Fire* used this statement to describe its author. Despite the overwhelming experiences Elie has faced in life, he survived to become a spokesman *for* man, never against man. All his writings bear this out. Indeed, his popularity with younger readers may well be due to his teaching that it is possible to affirm life, even in these days. Not easy perhaps, but one has to try. "Man owes it to himself to reject despair," Elie says, finding this answer in his own background.

Hasidism teaches the importance of living in and enjoying the present, no matter what lies ahead. And of investing each act of life with beauty, for ourselves and for others. Elie believes it is this concern for his fellow-man which has kept the Jew alive . . . and human.

At New York's City College, Elie's course on the Holocaust has been drawing large crowds of students ever since it was first offered in the early 1970's. Many of his students are themselves children of survivors, and Elie suspects that they often take his course as much to understand their parents' fears and reactions as to understand the past.

Elie loves young people. He believes in them and feels he understands them. Their sensitivities and feelings have not yet been worn down by the cares and problems of daily living. He aims his writings chiefly toward the young; his message is directed to the hope of tomorrow. The youngsters whose singing and dancing he witnessed in the Soviet Union restored his optimism in a future for Soviet Jewry, but he worries about Jewish youth in the West in an era of drug culture and religious cults.

In the classroom, Elie Wiesel the public figure is left outside, on the other side of the door. Outside, too, is left the hectic pace, the strenuous schedule of flights, appearances, and interviews. Elie sits at his desk in the lecture room, his head cupped in his right hand, watch dial facing him, or he joins his students in a circle, collar loosened, tie askew—and he is Reb Eliezer, their Tzaddik.

Some days, he finds it as difficult to conduct class as it is for his students to attend it. The subject of the Holocaust drains both teacher and student emotionally. The pain is great, and it is torment to realize the depth of evil of which man is capable. Sometimes, when Elie reads heartbreaking material to them, tears well up in the eyes of his students. They hear details which they never heard at home, because their parents wished to protect them. But they feel they must know. They want to face what their parents went through.

Elie is aware of their feelings. "For them, as for me, the study of the Holocaust is not a course like any other. They come to it as a sacred initiation."

It is such a great responsibility to teach a course like this. Elie does not take it lightly. He knows the impact his words have on his students, how seriously they take what he teaches them in class. And he is concerned that they might be left with fears and anxieties which will overwhelm them.

Class discussions become heated, even bitter, at times. Students wonder out loud how their parents could marry, even put children into the world, after all the hatred they have gone through. Why did they have me? is the question many ask.

This is a point of great concern to Elie. More than even his students realize, it has become a topic which touches his own life.

On June 6, 1972, Shlomo Elisha Wiesel is born. For Elie, the arrival of his son was an event of immense personal joy filled with profound spiritual meaning.

It was for Elie the ultimate expression of Jewish faith to have a child. It was an act of "supreme defiance"; it proclaims his hope in the future. He declared that he might not have dared to bring a new life into the world if he had not been Jewish. But he is a deeply religious man.

The birth of a child means many things to him: not only hope, but the chance to change destiny.

"When he was born, I felt very sorry for him," Elie told a reporter. "I felt sorry for him coming into this ugly, difficult, horrible world. Now I still feel sympathy, but naturally the urge is much stronger than before to try to do what we can to make it a little better. Because he is here, we try."

Now Elie's view of himself as a link in the long history of the Jewish people also includes the next generation: "I was the only son. I cannot break the chain. It is impossible that 3,500 years should end with me, so I took these 3,500 years and put them on the shoulders of this little child."

For Elie, the naming of his son is particularly touching. He never forgets that over a million Jewish children were lost in the Holocaust, and because so many names were lost, he believes that each Jew should give his child more than one name.

In the living room of the Wiesels' Central Park West apartment, where the circumcision ceremony is celebrated on the eighth day after his arrival, the little boy receives the name of Elie's father. He becomes Shlomo ben Eliezer—Shlomo, son of Eliezer.

Among the guests present when the baby is blessed and named is a Hasidic rabbi, who turns to Elie and comments: "A name has returned." Elie's eyes are moist. Someday his son will be called up to the Torah to read, and the boy will be called by the same name that his own father bore when invited up to the Torah in the synagogue in Sighet. Shlomo Wiesel's family was destined to survive.

When he looks at his son, Elie often notices gestures and mannerisms which remind him strongly of that other Shlomo, his father. There is pain in the reminder, but there is also joy. The little boy is a living symbol to Elie that his father has not been forgotten. Another human being has entered the world to carry on his name.

23

In his novel *The Oath*, published in 1973, Elie records in a new way his inner struggle between "being afraid to speak" and "being afraid of keeping silent." The book's essence lies in the paradox which has troubled its author from the moment he began writing. In fact, even before he ever put words on paper he had fought the battle between "I cannot write about it" and "How can I not write about it?"

The Oath is the story of the village of Kolvillag, which is destroyed, and its people all killed, in a pogrom started by a false rumor blaming the local Jews for the death of a Christian boy.

Mad Moshe, familiar to readers of Elie's works, has become the village hero because of his attempt to save the village by sacrificing himself as the scapegoat for the alleged crime. Moshe senses that the pogrom will take place regardless of various attempts by others to head it off. When his sacrifice is not accepted by the town officials, Moshe tries another approach. He tells the townspeople that in all their long history, Jews have never been able to stop inhumanity from being inhuman. Neither through words nor actions have they been able to change events intended to destroy them. So why not, this time, accept the inevitable in silence? The villagers agree. No one will ever know the terror of their last days, as they swear an oath to that effect. If anyone survives this

177

wholesale killing, he must never reveal what has taken place in Kolvillag.

Azriel, an old man, is that single survivor. He is the witness who has seen the end of the village. For fifty years he keeps his vow of silence; he does not reveal his hideous past. But one day, in a city far from his native Kolvillag, he is confronted by a choice. He has met a young man, disappointed by life, who wishes to kill himself. Azriel tries to talk him out of suicide, but seems to fail.

Finally, in a desperate measure, Azriel uses his last resort: he breaks his oath of silence. Relating the story of his village in all the details of its destruction and terror, he convinces the young man that his suicide would be murder, another murder added to the long list of murders committed in Kolvillag, and therefore, only a gift to death.

The survivor, the witness to death, has broken his oath. He has ended his silence. But in so doing, he has saved a life. And that, in Jewish ethics, is the most important deed of all.

Like all of Elie's writings, *The Oath* is filled with many levels of meaning. It is not difficult to find the obvious parallels between its story and the life of its author. And with his concerns regarding the use and aspects of silence. The specific question asked is, does one have the right to keep silent when the welfare of other human beings is involved?

On October 6, 1973, while religious Jews in all parts of the world were spending Yom Kippur Day in their synagogues, fasting and atoning for past misdeeds, imploring God to renew their lives for another year, news came that Israel had once more been invaded by its neighbors. This was a harsh blow to all who had believed that peace was possible, especially since it was thought that the Six-Day

War in 1967 had proven to Israel's enemies that she was strong enought to defeat them.

Elie had been working on a dramatic poem set to the music of the world-renowned French composer Darius Milhaud, and he hurried it through rehearsals. On the night of November 11, 1973, the cantata *Ani Maamin: A Song Lost and Found Again* was presented by the Brooklyn Philharmonia Orchestra in a world premiere benefiting the Israel Emergency Fund of the United Jewish Appeal.

Not a few in the packed auditorium were there because they were despondent and discouraged by world events and wondered whether Elie's new work could offer some shred of solace and hope.

Elie was the cantata's narrator that night; the dramatic poem also included a chorus and the voices of the three patriarchs, Abraham, Isaac, and Jacob.

The chorus set the mood:

> We believe, O God, in you first of all,
> In you above all.
> And also in him—
> The Messiah.

The narrator opened his story:

> In those days, even as the heart of the world was
> being consumed by the black flames of night, three
> angry old men appeared before the celestial court.
> Asking to be heard.

Each patriarch tries to move God with his tale. Abraham tells God of the faithfulness for which he was to be rewarded with survival, with the blessing of his children beyond the time of eternity.

Isaac reminds Him of his intended sacrifice on Mount Moriah, of his acceptance and his silence as a gift to God.

Jacob recalls a dream he had: a ladder reached into the sky as if it were a bridge, and at the end of it were promises, promises made by God to watch over Israel, His people.

All the angels join the patriarchs' tears with their own. But God remains unmoved. And silent.

Reciting the long litany of Jewish suffering, the patriarchs enumerate all the sites of their people's agony and slaughter, begging God to use His divine powers to save Israel's children and put an end to their overwhelming pain. They are met by silence. God rejects their plea by His silence.

Yet the patriarchs do not give up. Over and over they list their accusations. How can God be so cruel, uncaring? Why does He refuse to hear them?

Each of their statements is interspersed by their recitation of Ani Maamin, "I believe." This refrain turns out to be more important than their task of moving a silent God to help.

For, as one by one Abraham, Isaac, and Jacob step away from the presence of God, who has remained wrapped in silence, they know that even if God has forsaken them, they have not given Him up. They will continue to believe in Him, and that will be their salvation. In spite of God, they will retain their faith in Him. And for that they will be blessed. Ani Maamin.

> Auschwitz has killed Jews
> But not their expectation.

> May you be blessed
> Israel
> For your faith in God—
> In spite of God.

May you be blessed
Israel
For your faith in man—
In spite of man.

May you be blessed
Israel
For your faith in Israel—
In spite of man
And God.

As each patriarch steps away, he does not notice that a tear is clouding the eye of God. Finally God, "surprised by his people, weeps for the third time—and this time without restraint, and with—yes—love. He weeps over his creation—and perhaps over much more than his creation."

According to one member of the audience at the world premiere of *Ani Maamin*, "Jews and non-Jews wept during this search for God and this proclamation of God," sealed by the author's words of dedication:

For Shlomo-Elisha
Son of Eliezer,
Son of Shlomo,
Son of Eliezer . . .

Despite everything, the cold dark November night had become an evening of hope.

24

EVERY MONDAY EVENING the New York–
bound plane from Boston brings Elie home from a day at
Boston University, where he is Andrew Mellon Professor
of Religion. Teaching in Boston once a week has become
an important part of his life. As before at New York's City
College, his classes and seminars are a magnet. Students
from all over Boston and the outlying areas attend.
Together with Elie they analyze texts and study the great
writings of sacred literature.

On most Mondays on his way back to New York, Elie
feels good about the day he has just left behind. He enjoys
both the teaching and the response of his students to him;
he feels he is gaining more than he is giving. On one
particular late-afternoon flight, however, Elie stares
through the plane windows at the fluffy cotton clouds
tinged pink by the departing sun, and is sick at heart.

Those clouds hold a special meaning for him. All
through his adult years he has envisioned them as the
home of the lost souls for whom no cemeteries exist, a last
resting place for the victims of hate. In his books, clouds
have become a symbol for those who died. It seemed that
even this symbol was to be denied them.

On Monday mornings, after arriving at his office at
Boston University, Elie usually picks up a stack of mail
which has arrived for him during the week. Today, as
always, his briefcase, resting under the passenger seat,

holds some of that mail. Mixed in with the letters is a postcard:

> I recently completed reading "The Hoax of the Twentieth Century" and the professor who wrote the book claims that the six million is a total fiction, that no Jews were gassed or toasted in the ovens in German concentration camps, that there was nothing in German records to substantiate the Jewish claims, that the confessions were obtained under duress. I guess Hitler was right when he said the Jew is the master of the big lie.

Shocked and furious, Elie is aware that the postcard is only one signal that a new campaign of anti-Semitic hatred is being unleashed. There are many other indications that new racial intolerances are boiling up all over the world. A theory called "revisionism" is sweeping six continents. This theory denies that the Holocaust ever took place. Keystone of the hate-mongering is the book referred to in Elie's mail. Published in 1976 by Arthur R. Butz, a professor of electrical engineering at Northwestern University, *The Hoax of the Twentieth Century* attempts to "prove" that the camps, the gas chambers, the killings, all are lies, spread by Jews themselves.

Financed by wealthy hate groups, the theory is being spread by historians who seem unaware that their "scholarship" is being used deliberately by their sponsors to promulgate anti-Semitism.

The new poison is effective. At the United Nations, one ambassador declares publicly that the *Diary of Anne Frank* is in actuality a forgery. In Germany, a former SS judge writes a book explaining that the furnaces of Auschwitz were only the chimneys for the camp bakery, nothing else. A Philadelphia professor, known for his Nazi sympathies, declares that the Holocaust experience was invented by Jews to make money through blackmail.

As his plane nears its New York destination, Elie gathers his papers, deeply troubled. He is well aware of the power words carry. Long ago, his teacher warned him: "With words you can create either angels or demons. Be careful. Do not create demons. Create only angels; create only the good and the humane." What of the demons created by the other side?

Elie is angry about this new assault on the Jewish people. Why is it always the survivors who must prove that their experience with death was "real"? Where are the Allied soldiers who liberated the death camps, who saw what had happened there? Perhaps, he thinks, all the survivors should gather in one place at one time, to "prove" to the world that the Holocaust really took place . . .

The commuter plane descends into the twinkling lights of New York City. Elie thinks of the words he will use in defense of the stilled voices:

> This is our enemies' ultimate viciousness: to try to make people believe—and many already do—that the death factories never existed, that they were invented by the victims. . . . Are we really to debate these "charges"? Is it not beneath our dignity—and the dignity of the dead—to refute these lies? . . . But then, is silence the answer? It never was.

In *A Jew Today*, published in 1978, Elie's thoughts on "What Did Happen to the Six Million" are incorporated in a collection of essays, letters, diary excerpts, and memoirs. His testimony of a Jew's beliefs is set out here in the hope that "some writings could sometimes, in moments of grace, attain the quality of deeds."

The story of Dodye Feig appears here—Elie's portrait of his grandfather. Also detailed is Elie's first encounter with the Nobel laureate François Mauriac, who was destined to launch the stateless, orphaned young man on a writing career. Mauriac, in 1958, dedicated *The Son of Man*, his book on the life of Christ, in the following manner:

To
Elie Wiesel
Who was a crucified Jewish child
His friend
François Mauriac

Compassionate thoughts on the fall of Biafra in one article, great sympathy for the objects of South African apartheid in another, back up Elie's lead story: to be a Jew today does not mean one wants to convert the world to Judaism, but it does mean an attempt to save mankind from itself.

In "A Plea for the Survivors," Elie deals with those who were spared, but have left part of themselves in the Kingdom of Night. He knows them well, for he is part of that band. Like other survivors, he "walks one step above the ground," listening for sights and sounds he has experienced, not having words adequate to describe the event. None of the words being told will ever do it justice. The Holocaust has become the theme of books, plays, poetry, all sensationalizing the unspeakable. The writers have become commercial hits; their audiences undergo shock and pity at first, then become "turned off." It seems to the survivors that no one really listens, that no one has learned any lessons from their ordeal.

It is Elie Wiesel's view that all Jews alive today owe their lives to a certain grace. The very fact of their

survival, he believes, carries with it a number of obliga-
tions. As a Jew, one must bear witness. As a Jew, one must
be a link between the dead of the Holocaust and today's
world. As a Jew, one must be a link between the Jew and
the non-Jew.

Elie, whose life since the Holocaust has been devoted
to bearing witness, teaches and writes that the opposite of
love is not necessarily hate, but indifference. Indifference
is a sin; it makes one an accomplice. The recent experiences of the Jewish people prove how dangerous is the sin
of indifference.

When, in November of 1978, President Jimmy Carter
invited him to head the President's Commission on the
Holocaust, Elie accepted eagerly. The Commission's
purpose was to be the same as his goal had always been:
the need to remember. Under Elie's chairmanship, the
President's Commission on the Holocaust, and the Holocaust Memorial Council, which succeeded it, suggested
that a museum/study center might be an appropriate
American memorial to the victims of the Holocaust. Also,
certain annual "Days of Remembrance" were recommended to honor all who had lost their lives in the
Holocaust.

On April 24, 1979, the first such Day of Remembrance
was observed in the Capitol Rotunda in Washington,
D.C. The gathering included the President, the Congress, and hundreds of guests, who stood in silence as
Elie, slim and frail, his sensitive hands brushing back the
straggly hair from his forehead, addressed them.

Thirty-five years ago almost to the day, he said, a small
Jewish boy and his family, and all the occupants of their
town, were herded together and taken into exile. Thirty-
five years ago, the little boy and his father stood facing the
flames which were to devour most of the world they had
known, and the little boy asked his father whether this

Swearing-in Ceremony, Roosevelt Room, The White House, Washington, D.C., February 15, 1979.
Chairman of the President's Commission on the Holocaust, Elie Wiesel and Speaker of the House, The Honorable Thomas P. O'Neill, Jr.
The Bible being used is an eighteenth-century Jewish Bible which had belonged to a congregation in Heidelberg. It was liberated from Nazi looted material in the Offenbach Archives and is now in the Klau Library of the Hebrew Union College in Cincinnati.

Official Photograph, The White House, Washington, D.C., Billie B. Shaddix

Days of Remembrance, The Capitol Rotunda, Capitol Hill, Washington, D.C., April 24, 1979.
From left to right in the foreground: President Jimmy Carter, Chairman of the President's Commission on the Holocaust Elie Wiesel, Majority Leader of the Senate Robert C. Byrd, Vice President Walter F. Mondale, Speaker of the House Thomas P. O'Neill, Jr., Cantor Isaac Goodfriend of the Advisory Board to the President's Commission on the Holocaust.

was not a nightmare from which they would awaken. Certainly what they were seeing could not take place in the middle of the twentieth century in a civilized society.

"If this were true, the world would not be silent," Elie quoted the boy as saying. To which the father had answered, "Perhaps the world does not know."

"The world knew and kept silent," said Elie.

Now, thirty-five years later, the same boy who had seen the conflagration stood in the Capitol of the United States of America and thanked its President for remembering, and for asking other nations also to remember.

"No other country, and its government, besides Israel," said Elie, "has issued or heeded such a call."

Long tapers in a menorah were lighted: six candles to memorialize the six million dead Jews of the Holocaust, and a seventh candle in commemoration of the Armenian genocide victims whose memorial was also observed that day.

"Memory may perhaps be our only answer," stated Elie. "Our only hope to save the world from ultimate punishment, a nuclear holocaust."

Kaddish was said in the Capitol Rotunda. The voices of the many who joined in the Hebrew prayer for the dead reverberated strangely in the echoing chamber.

On July 29, 1979, a plane left Kennedy Airport, New York, for a flight to Europe. Aboard, fifty-seven members of the President's Commission on the Holocaust and its advisory board, together with their spouses, began a trip into the past.

Led by Elie, as chairman, the group included Marion Wiesel and seven-year-old Elisha, Professor Robert McAfee Brown, Bayard Rustin, Rabbi Alfred Gottschalk, Lily Edelman, and Professor Franklin Littell, among others.

The first stop was Warsaw. Once the pride of Polish Jewry, this city now contained only a pitifully small remnant of poor, aged Jews. Their number was barely sufficient for the prayer service held on the day of the Commission's arrival, which coincidentally fell on Tisha B'av, commemorating the destruction of the First Temple in Jerusalem in 586 C.E. and the Second Temple in 70 C.E. Elie's group went to the synagogue that night. In accordance with ancient custom, the people present turned over the benches, took off their shoes, and extinguished the lights. They sat on the ground and read the Lamentations of the prophet Jeremiah by the light of candles. All the Commission members who participated in this mourning ceremony, even the non-Jews, had an acute sense of being in a place emptied of its Jews and deliberately erased of all Jewish memories.

The next morning the Commission traveled to Treblinka, along a route where many prosperous small Jewish towns had once stood. Eight hundred thousand Jews had lost their lives in Treblinka. Now nothing remained of the camp, deliberately destroyed by the Germans before the end of the war. A stone monument symbolically split in half, with a shattered menorah decorating its top, serves as a memorial. Next to it, two huge stone slabs inscribed with the words "Never Again" in six languages was erected by the Polish government. All around it, hundreds of stones in all sizes and shapes bear the names of Jewish communities decimated by the enemy.

On the third day of their trip, the members of the Commission entered Auschwitz. All were overcome by pain at the sight of this deadliest of the extermination camps. For the five survivors in the group, there was only silence. No one could bear to utter a word. Returning to this place was a journey which words could not describe. Even prayers had no meaning here.

Close by was the reception center of Birkenau. Here, the survivors separated themselves from the rest of the group: with Elie in their center, the five linked arms. They walked shakily over ground which was still familiar to them. They stood on the platform where cattle cars had once discharged them. Seared by sorrowful memories, they tarried at the site where the gas chambers had once operated, where their dear ones had been lost to them.

Here, at the very spot which symbolized all their torment, Elie uttered the Shema Yisrael, the Jewish credo, "Hear, O Israel, the Lord Our God, the Lord is One." As he related to an interviewer afterward:

> It was a whisper. It wasn't a shout. And they all picked it up, first the five survivors, then fifty people. They all said, "Shema Yisrael." That was the only thing. And it was a moment that remains with you, one of the great moments in life. . . . It meant to me that, in spite of 2,000 years of suffering and persecution by all the forces of evil, and exile, there is still a Jew saying "Shema Yisrael." It was a defiance, not a submission.

The next stop, Russia, was Elie's first return there since the publication of *The Jews of Silence* in 1966. He was not welcome in Russia; only an official request from the White House brought about the granting of a visa for him.

When the Commission reached the site of Babi Yar, outside of Kiev, where 80,000 Jews had been massacred by the Nazis during the Ten Days of Awe in 1941, a shock awaited it. A new monument, a very impressive one, had been erected on the site where the victims had tumbled into the ravine and have been covered over by earth, but not a single word on the memorial mentioned that it was Jews who had been killed there. "Victims of fascism" and "350,000 Soviet citizens died," it was written. The word "Jew" did not appear.

On the morning after the Kiev visit, the group attended Sabbath services at Moscow's main synagogue. News of the presence of Elie Wiesel had spread. He was asked to give a brief message from the pulpit and was given the honor of participating in the service.

It was the Sabbath of Consolation, and the synagogue was filled to its capacity of 800 people. While he was reciting the Haftarah portion. Elie saw the lips of the hundreds of men before him moving in unison with his. When he returned the Torah to the Ark, Elie had Elisha walk at his side. At that point, the men who had surrounded them on the pulpit kissed the Torah, then reached for the child's hand and kissed it too. Perhaps it was a feeling of pleasure and hope at having such a young boy at their service that prompted the gesture; perhaps they wanted to express to Elie Wiesel how much he meant to them. It was a moment which confirmed to Elie that he had been right to bring his child on this searingly painful trip.

Denmark was the last European country visited by the study group. Because the action of Danish citizens had saved the lives of many Jews who might have otherwise been killed by the Nazis, the visitors presented a scroll of gratitude to the King of Denmark, expressing thanks for his "setting an example of what humanity could do if it would."

A scroll thanking Raoul Wallenberg, a Swedish diplomat whose courageous action had saved the lives of 30,000 Jews during the German occupation of Hungary, was presented to Wallenberg's sister. The young diplomat was

Moscow Synagogue, U.S.S.R., August 4, 1979.
Elie Wiesel and Son, Elisha

Courtesy of United States Holocaust Memorial Council

Presentation of the Report of the President's Commission on the Holocaust, The Rose Garden, The White House, Washington, D.C., September 27, 1979. Chairman Elie Wiesel, President's Commission on the Holocaust and President Jimmy Carter.

Courtesy of United States Holocaust Memorial Council

arrested by Soviet troops when they took over Hungary,
and he has since disappeared in the prisons of the Soviet
Union. Despite an announcement by the Soviets that
Wallenberg died in prison in 1947, there is heightened
interest in the rumors that he may still be alive.

Israel was the study mission's last stop. At Yad Vashem,
the national Israeli shrine for remembering victims of the
Holocaust, valuable lessons awaited the Commission
before a visit with the President of Israel ended the
journey.

"The murder of one group inevitably provokes more
murder," Elie stated in September 1979 at a White House
Rose Garden ceremony during which the work of the
President's Commission on the Holocaust ended. The
moral implications of the Holocaust remain universal, he
noted. They touch the fate of mankind and involve
persons living far away from Auschwitz, even those who
were still unborn at the time of the Holocaust.

These sentiments were uncannily borne out at a
strange encounter at a remote Thai border town named
Aranyaprathet on a hot February day in 1980 when Elie
joined marchers from many parts of the world in an effort
to bring food and medications into Cambodia.

Once he, too, had traveled over the earth, hungry and
alone. He knew how it felt to be faceless, voiceless, and
forgotten. He had never forgotten his past, so it was
natural for him to travel to Thailand, like the others who
arrived from France, Norway, Spain, Britain, the United
States. They came because they wanted to help, because
they wanted to point up a tremendous tragedy which was
happening here while the world turned its back once
again. Or perhaps they just wanted to show they cared.

Many internationally known people came to join the
"March for Survival" organized by the International
Rescue Committee and a French group, Doctors Across

Frontiers. Among the women in short-sleeved dresses were actress Liv Ullman and singer Joan Baez; the men in summer shirts included Russian activist Alexandre Ginzburg, Bayard Rustin, a son of Winston Churchill, and a host of European and American political and artistic personalities. The crowd of about 150 marchers had brought twenty trucks filled with cases of food and medications to ease the acute hunger and illness within Cambodia.

Now the marchers watched as two men and a woman stood on a small bridge, part of the border between Thailand and Cambodia, and pleaded with the guards to accept the supplies they had brought. From the other end of the bridge, blank faces stared back, pretending not to hear. When it became apparent that the border guards would not be moved, the marchers turned away and sat down in the middle of the road. Within sight of the armed soldiers at the Cambodian end of the bridge, they held a vigil.

For Elie, this day held a special, private meaning. Thirty-five years before, by the Jewish calendar, Elie had lost his father in Buchenwald. He still remembered waking up in the cold barracks of the German concentration camp that long-ago dawn, and the horror and helplessness he felt when he discovered that his father had died during the night, and that the body had been removed before he could say a final goodbye, or recite a prayer over him.

For Elie Wiesel, Holocaust survivor, it was important to be in Thailand this day.

"I came here because nobody came when I was *there*," he said to the *New York Times* reporter accompanying the marchers. "One thing that is worse for the victim than hunger, fear, torture, even humiliation, is the feeling of abandonment, the feeling that nobody cares, the feeling that you don't count."

For Elie Wiesel the Jew, it was appropriate to keep his father's memory alive even here, in this place, near a country where millions had lost their lives under the dictatorship of cruel leaders, where war and famine were daily killing more.

And so, along with nine other Jews whom he located among the marchers, Elie stood in the dust of a Thai road and recited the Kaddish, the Jewish prayer for the dead.

At Elie's side stood a young French physician who prayed with him. When, afterward, Elie turned to him and asked if he were in mourning, the young Frenchman replied that his own father had died some years ago, but it was not the anniversary of his passing. Why then, questioned Elie, had he recited Kaddish here, now?

The young man pointed across the border into Cambodia and answered, "I said it for them."

Elie could have embraced him.

The next morning, reported the *New York Times*, the twenty truckloads of food and medicine intended for Cambodian relief were turned over to the Thai Red Cross, for distribution among refugee camps on the Thai side of the border. Afterwards, the marchers made their way back to Bangkok, and from there to their homes.

Elie Wiesel was quoted as commenting: "Perhaps we cannot change the world, but I do not want the world to change me."

In October 1980, following its passage by both houses of Congress, the President of the United States signed into law a bill that called for the eventual building of a permanent Holocaust memorial-museum and the dedication of specific Days of Remembrance of Victims of the

Holocaust, to be held annually in perpetuity. At long last the work of the Holocaust Commission had borne fruit. As chairman of the newly established Holocaust Memorial Council, which succeeded the Commission, Elie was highly pleased.

As Elie once explained in a conversation with Dr. Harry James Cargas of Webster College, he has found that writing is an ongoing, never-ending process.

> When I finish a book, I feel physically exhausted. But I never finish it because I always smuggle into every book one sentence which is the substance of the next book—a Jewish tradition. When we finish reading the Torah on Simchat Torah, we must begin again the same Torah at the same session. We never finish, we never begin . . . it's a continuous process. Thus when I finish one book, I have already begun another.

This is well illustrated by the genesis of Elie's eighteenth book, *The Testament,* published in the spring of 1981. *The Testament* evolved out of a book Elie began in 1965 during his first visit to the Soviet Union. Set against the background of Stalin's mass slaughter of Jewish writers and poets in August 1952, it recounts the life of Paltiel Kossover, a fictional poet who deserted Judaism for Communism and now is awaiting execution. The story is intended as a message to Paltiel's son, Grisha, a deaf-mute who never knew his father; it is conveyed through letters, poems, and memoirs, and through the words of Zupanev, the stenographer at the prisoner's interrogations, who writes down all the evidence.

"I lived a Communist and I die a Jew" is the message Paltiel sends to his son. Grisha understands. "Truth, for a

Elie Wiesel with President Ronald Reagan at the National Civic Commemoration Ceremony of the Days of Remembrance, April 30, 1981, in
the East Room of the White House, Washington, D.C. *To the left:* Mr.
Sigmund Strochlitz, Survivor, Council Member, and Chairman, Days of
Remembrance Committee for the Council.

Honorary Chairman Elie Wiesel Addressing The World Gathering of Jewish Holocaust Survivors, in Jerusalem, Israel in June, 1981

Photograph by Florette Ungar

Jew, is to dwell among his brothers. Link your destiny to
that of your people," is the testament left him by his
father, and Grisha, following its intent, emigrates to
Israel.

A storyteller with a mission? A witness to the world events
through which he has lived? A writer seeking to jar the
conscience of man? Where will Elie Wiesel go from here?

As honorary chairman of The World Gathering of
Jewish Holocaust Survivors in Jerusalem in June 1981,
Elie saw a dream come true. Almost 7,000 participants
came to the reunion, bringing their children, pledging
together that the Holocaust was an event which "must
never be forgotten, never be repeated." Elie's plea, to the
younger generation especially, was to keep the memory
sacred, not to allow commercialism to tarnish it.

Within walking distance of Elie's New York apartment is a
brownstone building which he visits on some of the
Saturday mornings when he is in town. A few steps
downward lead into its basement level, then he enters a
small Hasidic house of prayer. Except for its New York
setting, it is much like the ones he knew as a child.

Not much attention is paid to Elie when he worships
here. The men who pray in this room know who he is and
treat him as an equal, not as a celebrity. Most of the
worshippers are refugees themselves, survivors of as-
sorted European death camps; many of them are older
than he. Elie feels at home in this shtibel; he can be at
ease here.

When he prays here, he remembers his youth. Sometimes he recalls the famous Rebbe of Wishnitz and the last
visit to him, which ended on such a strange note. Many
years later, Elie was to have an incredible encounter, a
sequel to that day so long ago.

A distant cousin of Elie's lived in New York. One day, Elie received a telephone call, asking him to come to his cousin's bedside at once. Concerned, he rushed to the hospital where the cousin was facing surgery. There, his relative asked him for a blessing before the operation.

Elie thought this extremely strange. His relative was far more religious than he. Why did he need *his* blessing?

When Elie asked him, the cousin replied: "Do you remember the last time you and your mother visited the Wishnitzer Rebbe, when your mother cried for weeks afterward?" Of course, Elie remembered.

That day, Sarah Wiesel had spoken to the cousin. Now, so many years later, Elie was to receive the answer his mother had never given him.

Sarah had asked the Rebbe questions about her son's future, and he had told her: "Sarah, daughter of David, I want you to know that one day your son will grow up to be a great man in Israel, but neither you nor I will be alive to see it."

Elie's cousin felt that such a revelation about Elie might help in his predicament; perhaps Elie's blessing would see him through surgery safely. He received the blessing, and recovered successfully.

Elie, however, was shaken up by the turn of events. He was convinced "that there is no accident in life; there are only encounters. He had to become sick and I had to be in New York just to find the answer to that question." He pondered often on the encounter, strangely touched by the knowledge of that prophecy of long ago.

At least twice a week, Elie steps out of his apartment house into the rapid traffic of Central Park West and hails a taxi to travel to Upper Manhattan. There he keeps a date with an old friend. In the study of Professor Saul Lieberman, across a long table strewn with heavy books, he faces

the man he considers the greatest living talmudist. Elie
has been Saul Lieberman's student for years, since
coming to New York in the 1950's. They study for two
hours, three hours . . . whatever time there is that day. It
is Elie's greatest pleasure: at every session he finds new
beauty, new humanity. Once upon a time, he envisioned
that his life would be that of a scholar . . .

Refreshed by the Talmud's ancient wisdom, Elie returns to his apartment. In his room, where books line the
walls to the high ceiling and crowd every available
surface, his typewriter waits for him. Elie has given up
hoping that his words will change people or influence
events, but words are his reason for existence. Because
every moment is precious, Elie feels compelled to put it
to good use. He is conscious that his time on earth, time
granted him by virtue of his survival, is a gift which must
be utilized to the fullest.

Frequently, while writing, Elie's eyes stray to the
framed black-and-white photograph which hangs on the
wall directly over his typewriter. A small wooden house—
the home of his family in Sighet. And he goes on writing
. . . a new novel, another book on Hasidism, a dissertation on the Talmud . . . because he is obsessed by the urge
to be a witness from the past, a warning voice to the
future.

Bibliography

Bettelheim, Bruno. *The Informed Heart*. New York: Macmillan Co., 1960.

Brée, Germaine. *Camus and Sartre: Crisis and Commitment*. New York: Delacorte Press, 1972.

Cargas, Harry James. *In Conversation with Elie Wiesel*. New York: Paulist Press, 1976.

Davidowicz, Lucy S. *The War Against the Jews: 1933–1945*. New York: Holt, Rinehart & Winston, 1975.

Herzog, Chaim. *The War of Atonement*. Boston: Little, Brown & Co., 1975.

Kamm, Henry. "Marchers With Food Get No Cambodian Response." *New York Times*, February 7, 1980.

Kissinger, Henry. *White House Years*. Boston: Little, Brown & Co., 1979.

Levin, Nora. *The Holocaust: The Destruction of European Jewry, 1933–1945*. New York: Thomas Y. Crowell, 1968.

Lifton, Robert Jay. *Death in Life: Survivors of Hiroshima*. New York: Random House, 1967.

Rosenfeld, Alvin H., ed., with Irving Greenberg. *Confronting the Holocaust: The Impact of Elie Wiesel*. Bloomington: Indiana University Press, 1979.

Wiesel, Elie. *Night*. New York: Avon, 1969.

———. *Dawn*. New York: Avon, 1970.

———. *The Accident*. New York: Avon, 1970.

————. *The Town Beyond the Wall*. New York: Avon, 1972.

————. *The Gates of the Forest*. New York: Avon, 1967.

————. *The Jews of Silence: A Personal Report on Soviet Jewry*. New York: New American Library, 1967.

————. *Legends of Our Time*. New York: Avon, 1970.

————. *A Beggar in Jerusalem*. New York: Random House, 1970.

————. *One Generation After*. New York: Random House, 1970.

————. *Souls on Fire: Portraits and Legends of Hasidic Masters*. New York: Random House, 1973.

————. *The Oath*. New York: Avon, 1974.

————. *A Jew Today*. New York: Random House, 1978.

————. *The Testament*. New York: Summit Books, 1981.